The I ♥ TRADER JOE'S® Party Cookbook

The I ♥ TRADER JOE'S® Party Cookbook

Delicious Recipes and Entertaining Ideas Using Only Foods and Drinks from the World's Greatest Grocery Store

Cherie Mercer Twohy

 **Ulysses Press**

TRADER JOE'S® is a registered trademark of Trader Joe's® Company and is used here for informational purposes only. This book is independently authored and published and is not sponsored or endorsed by, or affiliated in any way with, Trader Joe's® Company.

Published by
Ulysses Press
P.O. Box 3440
Berkeley, CA 94703
www.ulyssespress.com

ISBN: 978-1-56975-792-5
Library of Congress Catalog Number 2010925860

Printed in Canada by Transcontinental Printing

10 9 8 7 6 5 4 3 2 1

Acquisitions Editor: Keith Riegert
Managing Editor: Claire Chun
Editor: Lauren Harrison
Proofreader: Lily Chou
Production: Judith Metzener
Design: what!design @ whatweb.com
Cover artwork: berry shortcake, Mexican platter, rack of lamb, pizza/chicken/watermelon salad, berry tart © Kevin Twohy; olives © Steyno&Stitch/shutterstock.com; flower © Regina Jershova/shutterstock.com; baker © marinamik/shutterstock.com; cookbook page © Torsten Lorenz/shutterstock.com; design blocks © Denis Barbulat/shutterstock.com; Old World map © paulojgon/shutterstock.com; frame © Laschon Richard/shutterstock.com; border © Olan/shutterstock.com; food skewer © Vinata/shutterstock.com; balloon © Hal_P/shutterstock.com; glasses © dimon75/shutterstock.com
Interior photos: see page 233

Distributed by Publishers Group West

4766 0724 1/12

TABLE OF CONTENTS

ACKNOWLEDGMENTS

I spent a lot of time on the thank-you list for my first book, as it never occurred to me that I'd write more than one! I'd really like to just thank all those same folks again, but I guess that's not the way to do this.

I'm still shaking my head over how Ulysses Press reached out to me—I became a first-time author over the Internet! It's a crazy story, and one that I often tell at speaking engagements as an illustration that anything can happen in life. I have to pinch myself to believe that I'm finishing my second book, and I have Keith Riegert and Lauren Harrison to thank for making the process (relatively) painless. Their support and enthusiasm for both books have been a great source of encouragement.

I have met so many amazing "Joe's" over the years, and they have been upbeat and positive about their jobs. How many corporations can you say that about these days? I thank everybody in the organization for all the great stuff they find, sell, and support, and for the fun stores to shop in. Keep on growin', folks!

I honestly cannot thank the students of Chez Cherie enough. They have stuck by us through thick and thin, in times of economic boom and bust! I'm overwhelmingly grateful for the friendship, positivity, and "cheerleading" we've enjoyed from our fabulous students.

My staff at Chez Cherie has not changed much over the years, and for that I am so very grateful. I'm blessed with a rock-star team of amazing women, and without them, my cooking life would be flat and flavorless. Chris Delgado, GeGe Engwald-Parry, Whitnee Haston, Valerie Barth, and Kareen Rowe have been by my side in classes and in life for years, and I'm so thankful to each of them. Chris and Whit worked on the prep and styling for the photo shoots on this book, which was such a huge help! Our "girl power" has extended to the scullery for the past few years, and our dishwashers, most often Gretchen and Anna, have kept our dishes sparkling—even the dreaded soufflé ramekins—with good humor. Thanks, ladies!

What would we do without friends? I'm blessed with too many to name (and terrified of omitting someone). Hugs and gratitude to all, for your support, encouragement, advice, and love. Right back at'chya.

And finally, my family. I'm not a gambler, because I used up all my good luck in the kid lottery. Steve and I are the luckiest parents on the planet, and Matt (who helped prep and style the photos for the book), Kevin (who took the awesome food shots), and Brenna (who's gonna write her own book someday) are the best, smartest, funniest, and most all-around fabulous humans I could have hoped to have in my life. Having that trio around is always my greatest joy. Love ya, kiddos.

⊙ INTRODUCTION

*I*f this book is in your hands, I'm going to assume that you're a fan of Joe's. And parties.

And those two are a dynamic duo, for sure. You don't always need to make a list of lists, cross-check, and color-coordinate in order to entertain. If that were the case, I'd never see my friends! You can pop into your local TJ's and bounce out of there 20 or 30 minutes later with your reusable bags bulging with party-fixings, no matter what the occasion. That makes celebrating a breeze, and we could all use some more celebrating in our lives, right? So whether you have a promotion to crow about, or you're just relieved to have made it to Friday, I hope the ideas in this book will spark the desire to call (or text—does anybody call anymore?!) a few friends and share a meal or great snacks together.

Here's a little personal information about me: I always have shrimp in my freezer, and I always have a bottle of bubbly in my fridge. That means I'm party-ready, 24/7. And while I don't feel like a one-woman fiesta every minute, I like living my life knowing that if cause for celebration arises, I'm equipped for success. In fact, while I'm in the confessional, I will disclose that I also carry a wine-opener and a cheese knife in my purse at all times—unless I'm about to subject myself to airport security. Absolute fact. Why? Because wine and cheese emergencies are the kind I like to be prepared for. Other girlfriends have pepper spray or bandages or stain remover in their Kate Spades, but I'm the one to turn to in a party emergency. I can't tell you how many times these two tools have come in handy. You should see the awed look of amazement that results when the need arises and I whip out that corkscrew. I think I've inspired more than one person to adopt the same purse necessities over the years.

Whether you're planning a "save the date," engraved-invitation-with-actual-postage-stamp event, or a supercasual, spur-of-the-moment Netflix night, this book has menu ideas to get you started on a year of memorable evenings with your best buds. (Please check out my first book, *The I Love Trader Joe's Cookbook*, for even more quick and tasty menu ideas.) By all means, mix and match them—these are party-sparking ideas, not set-in-stone rules. The flying monkeys won't swoop in to carry you off if you serve the Martini Madness menu on Super Bowl afternoon. In fact, I strongly encourage you to take a "one from column A, one from column B" approach to using these suggestions. I've bundled the recipes into party menus that I might serve, but by no means does this dictate that they should always be linked together!

Not only do I encourage you to mix and match the recipes for your signature party menu, I hope you'll play with the ingredients, too. In my cooking classes at Chez Cherie, I really try to encourage confidence in my students so that they'll know that swapping one tapenade for another, or using cherry preserves in place of apricot, will rarely result in anything inedible. (And if it does, have a good laugh and pop a TJ's frozen pizza or Tarte d'Alsace in the oven!) That makes them much more confident in the kitchen, which is the goal of cooking classes, isn't it? It gives them permission, in a way, to deviate from what's on the written recipe page, and to make that dish their own. While we may not have shared a kitchen, I hope you'll have the courage to tweak these recipes a little and make them yours. It's good to have a few "hows and whys" as a foundation, so a few basic cooking classes are a great investment in your culinary future.

These event ideas are, for the most part, arranged in calendar order. So, if you decide to make the Sweetheart Dinner menu in June, you won't find blood oranges on your TJ's produce shelves. No worries—kitchen improv is fun, puts you in touch with seasonality, and may result in a terrific culinary creation. It's so fun to experiment with different ingredients, and it makes the whole process more creative and personal. Also, if you're a frequent TJ's shopper, you're well aware that ingredients come and go like middle-school crushes around there. The tapenade I recommend while writing this book may be long gone by the time you get around to trying that recipe. It's the joy and curse of Trader Joe's. They're always finding great new stuff, but since the store walls aren't made of Silly Putty, they don't have room to stock it all. So, something's gotta give. And sometimes those decisions about discontinuation can break our hearts. Believe me, I've shopped there forever, and my heart has been broken so many times, I think Joe and I need a little couple's therapy. (Sniff, sniff—Hot and Sweet Mustard. Stifled sob—frozen puff pastry!)

While we're on the subject of all those great products, I just want to point out that this is a cookbook, so I've given you recipes for cooking (and a little bartending)…but by all means, take one or two of the recipes out of a themed menu and replace them with pre-prepared goodies from TJ's. If a special occasion rolls around and you're not prepared with a three-course feast, swan-shaped napkins, and a signature cocktail, never fear. No sense stressing yourself when there are appetizers, entrées, and desserts just waiting to be invited to the party, or bottles of something bubbly just waiting to be popped open! (You're on your own for the swans, though.) In the "Grab and Go" boxes, I've made suggestions to fit some of the themes so you're celebration-ready any day of the year, but of course, it's your party—you know what you and your friends love to eat!

Unless otherwise noted, I've written these recipes to serve four. I know that's a small party, but those are sometimes the best kind. Also, I'm math-challenged, and for my like-minded brethren out there, I think that's the easiest math to do—scale the recipe up by half, and you can serve six, double it and you'll have enough for eight, triple things for twelve. It seems like the simplest math to me! A few recipes, like the Guinness and Coffee Cupcakes (page 79), make more than you'll need for four. Most drink quantities are for a single serving, but most can be made in quantity by increasing each ingredient appropriately.

The beverage suggestions for each party are just that—as I always say, drink what you like! For example, I'm not a brown-liquor girl, but your gang may be big on bourbon. Know your audience. Of course, you'll want a nonalcoholic offering for your gathering, as well as more licentious libations. Here are two terrific reference books I recommend if you're stuck on what to serve, drinkwise: *What to Drink with What You Eat* by Andrew Dornenburg and Karen Page (Bulfinch, 2006) and *Drink This: Wine Made Simple* by Dara Moskowitz Grumdahl (Ballentine Books, 2009). Both are full of info and guidance, and both are terrifically written. I kept both as bedside reading for a while, until I got too thirsty!

So, if you've got the tiniest little thing to celebrate, cheers! Pop a cork, raise a glass, and serve a platter of something yummy—I'm raising my glass in salute to your celebrations!

If you create something terrific using one of these recipes as your springboard, I'd love to hear about it! You can reach me at cherie@ilovetraderjoes.com.

WORKING YOUR JOE'S: STRATEGIES FOR GETTING THE BEST OUT OF YOUR TRADER JOE'S® EXPERIENCE

● **HOARD YOUR FAVORITES.** Hoarding is an ugly word, but sometimes ya gotta. Most of us have experienced the Heartbreak of TJ's when that staple ingredient, be it mustard, puff pastry, or a particularly delicious mojito sauce, suddenly disappears from the shelf, leaving devoted customers feeling bereft. I've been shopping at Trader Joe's so long that I've been down this Heartbreak Road many, many times. So now, when I find some new shelf-stable or freezable item that I fall in love with, I purchase two or three. I use those and replace them as I do, so I've always got a couple in reserve in case there's a supply problem and my TJ's is out for a week or two. I also watch the shelves for signs of change. If my favorite salsa usually has a "four-jar-across" placement and I notice that it has diminished to two, I get nervous. I'll see if I can find out why it's in short supply, and if I can't, I'll grab a few extra jars, just in case.

● **MAKE FRIENDS WITH YOUR "JOES."** It's easy to do because they're friendly by nature. When I visit a TJ's, I often pay attention to the crew, and they're nearly always smiling, chatting, and offering help. Frequently, I'll pass a crew member in the aisle, and he or she will ask, "Can I help you find something?" (Not sure whether I look particularly helpless, but it's still nice.) I've overheard crew members deftly handle some very difficult customers with aplomb; they really do aim to please. Once you've established a relationship, your friends at TJ's will alert you to new stuff they think you might like. If you need something in quantity, call ahead and they'll set it aside for you—not that they wouldn't do that anyway, but it's just more like dealing with a mom 'n' pop merchant if you're on a first-name basis.

● **CHECK OUT THE WEBSITE.** There's been a terrific improvement in the Trader Joe's website in the past few years: tons of dietary information, new product blurbs, and even recipes. (Hey! That's my job!) If there's a recall on an item, you can read about it not only at the checkout counter, where signs are posted, but also on the website. You can also read about TJ's lore, find store locations, and even talk back to Joe! E-mail your questions or fill TJ's in on your joys (at a new product that has rocked your world) or sorrows (I can't live much longer without the Hot and Sweet Mustard!). I've been told by Trader Joe's insiders that they do take customer requests very seriously, so let 'em know what you're thinking.

● **GO TO "THE ALTAR."** The folks up there *know stuff*. Rather than ask a crew member who's stocking shelves about a product, head up to the front desk and ask someone there. They have access to a computer list that will give you the straight scoop on whether something is held up at a port of entry (which happened during the Great Caper Shortage of '08), or TOS (temporarily out of stock), or the dreaded DISCONTINUED. If something you love and need has been (horrors!) given the big "D" (and it *is* a sort of divorce, sometimes—painful and sudden, and you feel helpless and alone), ask for the flier that contains addresses and phone numbers for all the TJ's locations. Zero in on the ones in your "willing to drive there" zone and call them. (I'm a little embarrassed to admit that I have more than two TJ's on my speed dial.) If they have some of your beloved item in stock, they'll hold it for you. Me? I'm not a "cold turkey" kind of girl. I need to wean myself from my current favorite pasta shape or vinegar. So I grab what I can, and each time I open a package, I remind myself that this is nearly the end of this particular love affair and soon it will be time to move on to another great product.

● **THINK OUTSIDE THE FROZEN-FOOD BOX.** Just because it says frozen carrots doesn't mean you can't use it in a million ways. Think about the ingredient, not the finished product. Don't look at that frozen brown rice just as a microwavable side dish—think of it as a head start on fried rice (using up the remnants of several bags of frozen veggies and the last egg in the carton), or as an add-in to make leftover soup heartier and more healthful.

● **WATCH THE DISPLAYS FOR NEW ITEMS AND "HUSTLE BUYS."** This is a good way to find a great new snack or salad dressing or grab a terrific bottle of Hustle Buy wine or beer at a fantastic price before it's going-going-gone.

● **LISTEN TO OTHER CUSTOMERS AND ASK QUESTIONS.** Trader Joe's is a friendly place, so they'll probably be happy to help. If you see someone putting eight boxes of curry sauce in her cart, ask what fabulous dish she has in mind. Not only will you get a great recipe idea, you might also make a friend. After all, you have a discerning appreciation of Trader Joe's in common.

NEW YEAR'S DAY

- COWGIRL CAVIAR
- GOOD LUCK GREENS AND BEANS
- CRISPY-CHEESY POLENTA ROUNDS
- BAKED GINGER-BOURBON PEARS
- TANGERINI

After a busy party season, the most festivity I can muster by New Year's Day is a low-key afternoon of parade and bowl-game watching, with accompanying munchies. Here's a no-stress menu that can serve as a lazy lunch, or stretch on into the evening if the game goes into overtime. You can start your healthy eating resolutions off right with this meal, if you hold the ice cream on dessert! If you want to augment this almost-no-meat menu, add a roasted chicken (either home-roasted or grabbed from the prepared food section at your TJ's).

COWGIRL CAVIAR

I made a test version of this dish and took it to a girl's night. On the drive home, I found myself scooping up the leftovers at each stoplight. Not sure if that's as bad as texting while driving, but surely it's not recommended. But it does show you how tasty this stuff is!

1 (15-ounce) can black beans, drained and rinsed

1 (11-ounce) package steamed black-eyed peas, rinsed

1 cup coarsely chopped Trader Joe's Mixed Medley Cherry Tomatoes

1 (13.75-ounce) jar Trader Joe's Corn and Chile Tomato-Less Salsa

6 green onions, chopped

3 to 4 tablespoons minced jalapeño

¼ cup chopped cilantro

2 tablespoons olive oil

3 to 4 tablespoons red wine vinegar

salt and pepper

corn chips or Reduced Guilt Multigrain Chips, for dipping

DO AHEAD
VEGAN, GLUTEN-FREE
(if served without chips)

Toss everything together in a large bowl. Adjust seasoning to taste—more jalapeño if you like it hotter, more vinegar if you want more tang.

Prep Time: 5 minutes

This makes more than enough for four, but it's great stuff to have around. In fact, it's better the next day. It makes a terrific omelet or quesadilla filling, and it's good for you, too! You can customize this to your heart's content—avocado cubes, chopped red onion, garlic...add, subtract, and make it your own!

GOOD LUCK GREENS *and* BEANS

Eating greens at New Year's is supposed to put green in your wallet all year. The cooked greens resemble crumpled cash, and the bounty of beans represents abundance.

2 tablespoons olive oil

1 red onion, sliced into half-moons

3 cubes frozen garlic

1 (16-ounce) bag Trader Joe's Southern Greens Blend, coarsely chopped

2 cups vegetable or chicken broth

1 (12-ounce) package Chicken Andouille or another spicy cooked sausage, sliced (optional)

1 (16-ounce) can cannellini beans, drained and rinsed

salt and pepper

red chile pepper flakes

DO AHEAD
VEGETARIAN *(if made without sausage)*, **GLUTEN-FREE**

In a large sauté pan, heat the olive oil and sauté the sliced red onion until fragrant, about 4 minutes. Add the garlic and sauté 1 to 2 minutes. Add half the chopped greens and sauté until they wilt down enough to add the rest. Sauté until all the greens are wilted. Add the broth and simmer until the greens are tender, about 10 minutes. Add the sliced sausage, if using, and stir to warm through. Add the drained beans and toss to incorporate. Adjust seasonings to taste.

Prep Time: 10 minutes
Cooking Time: 25 minutes

CRISPY-CHEESY POLENTA ROUNDS

These golden disks of corny goodness make a great base for the Good Luck Greens and Beans. They're also terrific with meaty pasta sauce, a poached egg, or some spicy cooked sausage. I guess what I'm trying to say here is that they're just good—by themselves, or with other stuff!

2 teaspoons butter

1 (18-ounce) roll Trader Joe's Organic Polenta, cut into ½-inch rounds

1½ cups shredded cheese (Trader Giotto's Quattro Formaggio, Trader Joe's Smoked Shredded Cheese Blend, or any shredded cheese you like)

VEGETARIAN, GLUTEN-FREE

In a nonstick skillet, melt the butter over medium heat. Working in batches, brown the polenta rounds, about 3 minutes per side. Sprinkle a little cheese on each round, flip over and cook until the cheese melts into a lacy, crisp layer. Remove to a platter, cheese sides up, and continue until all rounds are cooked.

Prep Time: 5 minutes
Cooking Time: 15 minutes

GRAB & GO
No-Prep New Year's Day

You may be shopped out by New Year's, but a quick trip to TJ's can fill your fridge and start the year off right! Grab these yummy treats from the frozen section:

- PASTRY BITES, LIKE CARAMELIZED ONION AND FETA
- CREAMY SPINACH-ARTICHOKE DIP
- MANY GREAT VARIETIES OF FROZEN PIZZAS

BAKED GINGER-BOURBON PEARS

The triple-play of ginger, bourbon, and pear flavors is a great combination. The soft sweetness of the pears, the zing of the ginger, and the smoky bourbon notes come together in delicious harmony. Add some cold, creamy ice cream, and the new year is off to a terrific start!

3 tablespoons butter

3 tablespoons chopped candied ginger

1 tablespoon bourbon

½ cup brown sugar

3 pears (D'Anjou or Bosc are good choices)

¼ cup chopped pecans or hazelnuts

vanilla ice cream or dollops of crème fraîche

**DO AHEAD
VEGETARIAN, GLUTEN-FREE**

Preheat oven to 400°F. Dot the butter over the bottom of an ovenproof casserole dish. Mix the chopped candied ginger, bourbon, and brown sugar together and sprinkle over the butter. Peel and core the pears and cut them into 6 to 8 wedges each. Place them on top of the brown sugar and bake until nearly tender, 15 to 30 minutes (depending upon the ripeness of the pears). Turn the pears to coat them with the sauce, and cook another 5 to 10 minutes, until glazed. Sprinkle with chopped nuts and serve with vanilla ice cream or crème fraîche.

Prep Time: 10 minutes
Cooking Time: 30 minutes

TANGERINI

Of all the juices on the refrigerated shelves, the tangerine is my very favorite. I just love the tangy yet honeyed flavor, and the sunny color. And Champagne? Well, in my book, that's always a good plan.

FOR EACH DRINK:
tangerine juice
champagne
tangerine slice, for garnish

Fill a champagne flute one quarter full of tangerine juice. Carefully top off the glass with champagne or another sparkling wine. Garnish with a tangerine slice.

SICILIAN IDYLL

- RICOTTA AND CAPONATA CROSTINI
- MEATBALL MINESTRA
- SICILIAN LEMON SALAD
- PENNE DI PISTACHE
- TORTA DELLA NONNA
- ITALIAN LEMON DROP

I don't think I've ever met anyone who doesn't like Italian food. Maybe that's because there's such a wide spectrum from which to choose. I recently had the pleasure of accompanying a group of students to Sicily, where we had an utterly amazing experience. The people, the food, the sparkling Mediterranean—it was a trip I'll never forget. These recipes are Sicily-centric, but you could easily assemble a Northern Italian menu using Trader Joe's polenta, sauces, and breads.

RICOTTA and CAPONATA CROSTINI

I confess that I'm not a huge eggplant fan. It's a texture thing. But in Sicily, I think we had eggplant at least twice a day, and I succumbed to its silken charms. This jarred caponata has a fresh flavor that pairs beautifully with the creamy ricotta. Mangia bene!

½ (19-ounce) jar
Eggplant Caponata

½ baguette, cut into rounds

½ (15-ounce) container
ricotta cheese

DO AHEAD
VEGETARIAN

If desired, pulse the caponata in a food processor to make the eggplant chunks smaller. Toast the bread, if desired. Spread about a tablespoon of ricotta on each baguette round and spoon a little caponata on top.

Prep Time: 5 minutes

MEATBALL MINESTRA

This soup has it all—super-fast and easy to throw together, looks terrific, it's good for you, and it tastes sooo good! That's a winning combination in my book.

3 cups chicken broth

1 (12-ounce) package Trader Joe's Gourmet Chicken Meatballs with Sun-Dried Tomatoes, Basil, and Provolone

handful of arugula

salt and pepper

Toscano Cheese with Black Pepper, for garnish

DO AHEAD
GLUTEN-FREE

In a saucepan, bring the broth to a boil. Add meatballs and simmer until warmed through, about 5 minutes. Add arugula and cook 2 to 3 minutes to wilt. Season to taste with salt and pepper. Ladle into bowls and grate some cheese over each portion.

Prep Time: 5 minutes
Cooking Time: 10 minutes

SICILIAN LEMON SALAD

Sicilian lemons are world famous (and world envied). Meyer lemons are their stand-ins in this dish. A regular lemon would be too tart to eat in this manner, but the sweetness of the Meyer lemon works well in this vibrant and unusual salad.

2 Meyer lemons

1 (4-ounce) bag mâche lettuce or ½ (7-ounce) bag arugula

½ red onion, thinly sliced

2 green onions, thinly sliced

¼ cup olive oil

salt and pepper

VEGAN, GLUTEN-FREE

Cut both ends off the lemons. Set a lemon on one end on a cutting board, and using a paring knife, follow the curve of the lemon from top to bottom, cutting off the peel and pith. Repeat with the other lemon. Cut between the membranes, removing the segments of flesh from both lemons. Reserve extra juice from the membranes. Toss the greens with the onions and lemon segments. Lightly salt the salad ingredients, then add any reserved lemon juice and olive oil and toss again. Adjust seasoning to taste with salt and pepper.

Prep Time: 10 minutes

PENNE DI PISTACHE

This was one of my favorite pasta dishes in bella Sicilia. *I loved the unusual use of pistachios in the sauce and the pretty green sprinkle of the nuts on top of the pasta.*

1 pound penne, cooked al dente and drained (reserve about 1 cup of pasta water)

1 tablespoon butter

1 cup finely chopped onion

¼ cup cubed pancetta

½ cup cream

¼ cup finely chopped pistachios, plus extra, coarsely chopped for garnish

salt and pepper

grated Parmesan cheese (optional)

Cook the pasta and reserve about 1 cup of the cooking water. In a sauté pan, heat the butter and sauté the onion until fragrant, 3 to 4 minutes. Add the pancetta and sauté 2 to 3 minutes. Add the cream and finely chopped pistachios, and simmer 5 minutes. Add the penne to the sauce and toss to coat. Add a little of the reserved pasta water if a saucier consistency is desired. Season with salt and pepper, and garnish with coarsely chopped pistachios and a little Parmesan, if desired.

Prep Time: 5 minutes
Cooking Time: 15 minutes

TORTA DELLA NONNA

There are as many versions of this pine-nut-and-ricotta dessert as there are nonnas *(Italian grandmas). Some are more like a cheesecake, but I love this double-crusted pielike treat.*

PASTRY:

3 tablespoons butter

3 tablespoons olive oil

2 cups flour

1 whole egg

2 egg yolks

½ cup sugar

½ teaspoon vanilla

FILLING:

1 (15-ounce) container whole-milk ricotta cheese

½ cup pine nuts, plus extra for garnish

½ cup sugar

zest and juice of 1 lemon

3 eggs

powdered sugar, for garnish

DO AHEAD
VEGETARIAN

FOR PASTRY: Preheat the oven to 375°F. In a small saucepan, melt the butter with the olive oil. Cool to room temperature.

In a food processor, combine the flour, whole egg, egg yolks, sugar, vanilla, and cooled butter and olive oil mixture. Process just until the pastry resembles coarse meal. Place on a lightly floured surface and knead until smooth. Refrigerate 10 minutes. Divide the dough in half, and roll out each half into a 10-inch round.

FOR FILLING: In the food processor, combine the ricotta, pine nuts, sugar, lemon zest, lemon juice, and egg until smooth.

Line a 9-inch removable-bottom tart pan with one of the dough rounds, arranging the excess dough up the sides of the pan. Spread the ricotta mixture evenly over this layer. Place the remaining dough over the top and pinch the edges of the top and bottom crusts together. Bake for 35 to 40 minutes, until golden. Garnish with more pine nuts and powdered sugar.

Prep Time: 15 minutes
Cooking Time: 45 minutes

• •

This dough can be as finicky as a Sicilian (or any other) toddler. Some days it rolls out beautifully, other times it will fight you. The good news? You can patch, press, and coax it into place, repeating the word *rustico* as you do so. In a pinch, use the Trader Joe's Gourmet Pie Crust (it doesn't have olive oil in it, but who will call you on that?) or a frozen Tiramisu Torte.

• •

ITALIAN LEMON DROP

Love-love-love the TJ's limoncello. I keep a bottle in the freezer at all times. It's also great over a scoop of sorbet or vanilla ice cream.

FOR EACH DRINK:
1 ounce vodka
1 ounce limoncello
2 ounces lemonade
splash of Grand Marnier

Pour ingredients over ice in a rocks glass.

SUPER BOWL

★ ● CHICKEN CHILI
● STUFFED SUB
● SUPER CHILE DIP

I confess that I have no sports gene. I can't tell a touchdown from a touchback (if that's even a thing). But I do enjoy the vibe when friends are cheering on their team, especially when they're enjoying a great array of grub while they do it. Of course, you can add your favorite prepared dips, salsas, or other purchased goodies to this menu—far be it for me to get between sports fans and their snack of choice!

CHICKEN CHILI

This is a bowlful of goodness, and it's even good for ya! It goes together quick and easy, and while it simmers, you can throw together the Super Chile Dip (page 34). Double or triple the batch if you have a bigger crowd, or if you want great leftovers!

1 tablespoon grapeseed or canola oil

1½ pounds boneless, skinless chicken, coarsely chopped (I like thighs, but you can use breasts, tenders, or a combination)

1 cup chopped onion

2 cubes frozen garlic

3 (15-ounce) cans beans (like black and/or kidney), drained and rinsed

1 (14.5-ounce) can chopped tomatoes

1 (4-ounce) can chopped Hatch Valley Fire-Roasted Diced Green Chiles

1 (12-ounce) container fresh salsa (in the refrigerated case)

2 tablespoons Trader Joe's Taco Seasoning Mix (or to taste)

3 cups chicken broth

salt and pepper, to taste

grated cheese, crème fraîche or sour cream, and chopped green onions, for garnish, if desired

DO AHEAD
GLUTEN-FREE

Heat the oil in a large stockpot. Working in batches, sauté chicken pieces in oil, just until they lose their pink color. As batches are cooked, remove them to a container and continue with remaining chicken. When all the chicken has been sautéed, return it to the stockpot. Add the onion, then the garlic, and sauté until aromatic. Stir in remaining ingredients. Bring to a boil, then reduce heat to a simmer. Stirring occasionally, cook about 30 minutes, until the chili reaches the desired consistency. Garnish as desired.

Prep Time: 10 minutes
Cooking Time: under an hour

STUFFED SUB

Wait 'til you try this—people go nuts for it. Whatever your sports passion is, I predict you'll make this sub all season long.

1 (18-ounce) loaf whole-grain bread

2 tablespoons olive oil

½ pound Italian sausage, removed from casings

½ pound ground turkey

1 cup onion, diced

4 cubes frozen garlic

1 cup Trader Giotto's Organic Vodka Pasta Sauce

1½ cup Trader Giotto's Quattro Formaggio (or other shredded cheese)

salt and freshly ground black pepper

DO AHEAD

Preheat oven to 400°F. Split the bread loaf horizontally and pull out the center of the bread, leaving a "shell" of crust. Place the bread from the center in a large bowl and crumble it with your fingers until you have coarse crumbs. In a medium sauté pan, heat the olive oil and crumble in the sausage. Cook until barely pink, then add the turkey, onion, and garlic. Sauté until meat is cooked through. Add the bread crumbs and sauté until toasted. Return mixture to the large bowl and combine with pasta sauce and cheese. Spoon the mixture into the bottom half of the loaf, compressing slightly. Top with the top half of the bread. Cover with foil and bake until heated through, about 15 minutes. Remove foil and bake another 5 minutes. Cool slightly before cutting.

Prep Time: 20 minutes
Cooking Time: 20 minutes

SUPER CHILE DIP

You can use this tricked-out queso for chips, veggies, or even to make a great cheese bread. Just slather it on some sourdough and pop under the broiler for a minute or two.

½ (7.5-ounce) container crème fraîche

½ (8-ounce) container mascarpone

2 cups Trader Joe's Pepper Jack Shredded Cheese Blend

1 (4-ounce) can Hatch Valley Fire-Roasted Diced Green Chiles

1 tablespoon Trader Joe's Taco Seasoning Mix

3 tablespoons sliced green onion

DO AHEAD
VEGETARIAN, GLUTEN-FREE

Preheat oven to 375°F. In an ovenproof casserole dish, stir together the crème fraîche, mascarpone, shredded cheese, green chiles, and taco seasoning. Place the casserole on a baking sheet (to contain any spill-over) and bake until bubbling, about 12 minutes. Stir in green onions and serve.

Prep Time: 5 minutes
Cooking Time: 15 minutes

GRAB & GO
No-Prep Super Bowl Snacks

You don't have to look far to find an armful of great snackables at Joe's. Here are a few suggestions to get you started.

- PUB CHEESE
- SALSAS, DIPS, AND CHIPS GALORE

From the frozen section:

- MINI TACOS
- SOUTHWEST CHICKEN QUESADILLAS

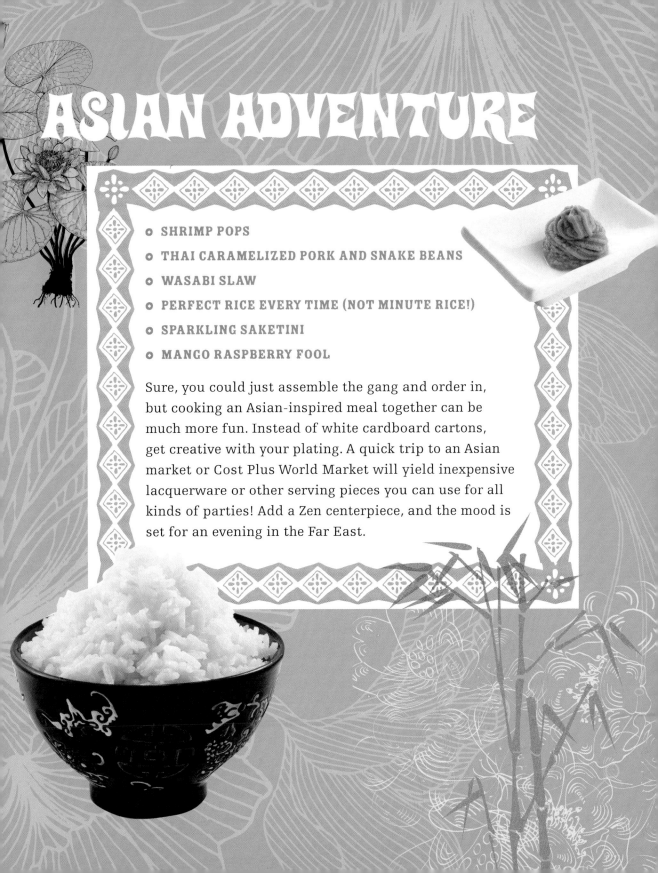

ASIAN ADVENTURE

- SHRIMP POPS
- THAI CARAMELIZED PORK AND SNAKE BEANS
- WASABI SLAW
- PERFECT RICE EVERY TIME (NOT MINUTE RICE!)
- SPARKLING SAKETINI
- MANGO RASPBERRY FOOL

Sure, you could just assemble the gang and order in, but cooking an Asian-inspired meal together can be much more fun. Instead of white cardboard cartons, get creative with your plating. A quick trip to an Asian market or Cost Plus World Market will yield inexpensive lacquerware or other serving pieces you can use for all kinds of parties! Add a Zen centerpiece, and the mood is set for an evening in the Far East.

SHRIMP POPS

These cute little pops are a great start to a meal—whether it's Asian-themed or not. The sweet chili sauce looks like a party in a bottle, and it brings such zip and tang! I love to use it with the frozen TJ's potstickers, too.

1 green onion, trimmed

2 cubes frozen garlic

1 teaspoon grapeseed oil

1 teaspoon soy sauce

pinch each of salt, pepper, and sugar

½ pound raw shrimp meat

1 egg white

Trader Joe's Sweet Chili Sauce, for dipping

DO AHEAD

Place the green onion and garlic in a food processor and chop coarsely. Add the grapeseed oil, soy sauce, salt, pepper, and sugar and pulse to combine. Add the shrimp and pulse to chop into a rough paste (with some chunks of shrimp remaining). Add the egg white and pulse to combine. Refrigerate mixture 30 minutes and soak bamboo skewers in water.

Working with a generous tablespoon of the mixture at a time, form a flat patty in one hand. (Slightly wet hands will help prevent the mixture from sticking.) Shape the patty around a soaked wooden skewer. Repeat with the remaining mixture. Refrigerate the shrimp pops 20 minutes. Preheat broiler and a broiler pan and place the pops on the hot pan. Broil 2 to 3 minutes, turn, and broil the other side.

Prep Time: 20 minutes
Cooking Time: 10 minutes

THAI CARAMELIZED PORK and SNAKE BEANS

I'm so excited that Trader Joe's has started to carry these cool beans. Call them snake beans, long beans, or yard-long beans—I just call them tasty! Sometimes I'll steam them whole and tie three or four in a big knot for a fun presentation. Drizzled with a little Black Pepper Sauce, they make a great side dish with big visual appeal.

1 bunch (about ¾ pound) snake beans, cut into 3-inch pieces

3 tablespoons soy sauce

¼ cup brown sugar

½ teaspoon red chile pepper flakes

2 teaspoons minced fresh ginger

1 tablespoon fresh lime juice

¾ pound pork tenderloin, cut into medallions, or pork loin chops, cut into strips

freshly ground black pepper

slivered red onion and chopped cilantro, for garnish

In a pot of boiling water, cook the snake beans until nearly tender, about 5 minutes. Drain and reserve.

In a medium sauté pan, combine the soy sauce, brown sugar, red chile pepper flakes, ginger, and lime juice. Bring to a boil, reduce heat, and cook a couple minutes, until the sauce is slightly thickened. Add the pork and snake beans to the pan and cook in the sauce until cooked through, about 4 minutes. If you need more liquid in the pan to prevent the sauce from burning, add a tablespoon or two of water. (The end result should be a thick, caramel-like sauce, but if you're nervous about burning the sauce, you can add water and then cook until the sauce re-caramelizes.) Season with black pepper. Place on a platter and garnish with slivered red onion and cilantro.

Prep Time: 10 minutes
Cooking Time: 15 minutes

• •

If snake beans aren't available, you can substitute fresh or frozen green beans.

• •

WASABI SLAW

This slaw is packed with crunchy veggies and looks great as a bed for lots of different entrées. Try it with roasted pork tenderloin or seared scallops.

¼ cup Trader Joe's Wasabi Mayonnaise

1 tablespoon seasoned rice vinegar

1 (10-ounce) bag broccoli slaw

handful of shredded carrots

handful of shredded cabbage

salt and pepper

DO AHEAD
VEGETARIAN, GLUTEN-FREE

For dressing, in a small bowl, stir together the mayonnaise and vinegar. Season lightly with salt and pepper.

In a large bowl, combine the broccoli slaw, carrots, and cabbage, and toss with dressing. Adjust seasoning with additional salt and pepper.

Prep Time: 5 minutes

If you like it less spicy, use 2 tablespoons Wasabi Mayo and 2 tablespoons regular mayo or crème fraîche.

GRAB & GO
No-Prep Asian Adventure

There are tons of ideas at TJ's for Asian-inspired celebrations! Here are just a few suggestions:

- SUSHI
- EDAMAME
- MISO SOUP

And from the frozen section:

- GYOZA POTSTICKERS (CHICKEN OR PORK)
- TEMPURA SHRIMP WITH SOY DIPPING SAUCE
- MOCHI ICE CREAM

PERFECT RICE EVERY TIME

Trader Joe's carries terrific pre-cooked, frozen white and brown rice. But as a cooking teacher, I put mastering rice-cooking on my list of mandatory kitchen skills for student success. This method is a great one to know!

3 cups water or chicken, beef, or vegetable broth

1½ cups long grain rice (jasmine or Basmati, for example)

DO AHEAD
VEGAN *(if made with water or vegetable broth)*, **GLUTEN-FREE**

Bring the liquid to a boil and stir in the rice. Bring liquid back to a boil and then reduce heat to very low. Cover the pan and simmer (on the lowest setting possible) for 15 minutes. When that time has elapsed, turn off the heat but do not lift the lid. Let the pan sit undisturbed for 5 minutes. Remove the lid and fluff the rice. Season as desired.

Prep Time: 5 minutes
Cooking Time: 20 minutes

If you've made the rice ahead of serving time, drape a clean kitchen towel over the top of the pan before you replace the lid. The towel will create a moisture barrier, preventing condensation from forming on the bottom of the lid and dripping back down onto the rice. This will keep the rice separate and fluffy, rather than sticky. Rice made this way in a heavy-bottomed pan will stay warm for about an hour. Be sure to keep the ends of the towel away from any burners you're still using—towel flambé is not a great culinary technique!

SPARKLING SAKETINI

I am deeply smitten with the TJ's Sparkling Sake bottles. A floral kimono–clad girl poses under a moon and star, and the little pull-tab opener is so clever!

FOR EACH SERVING:
½ bottle Trader Joe-san's Sparkling Sake

1 ounce Bombay Sapphire gin

cucumber or pineapple spear, for garnish

Pour a half bottle of the sparkling sake into a champagne flute. Add the gin and garnish with cucumber or pineapple.

MANGO-RASPBERRY FOOL

A fool, at least in the culinary world, is sweetened, puréed fruit with whipped cream. In my world, it's a way to use great, peak-of-flavor fruit to make a quick and gorgeous dessert. Use yogurt in place of the whipped cream and it's health food!

2 cups ripe mango cubes

juice of 1 lime

2 to 3 tablespoons honey or Trader Joe's Organic Blue Agave Syrup (or to taste, depending on sweetness of mango)

½ cup cream

½ pint raspberries

DO AHEAD
VEGETARIAN, GLUTEN-FREE

In a food processor or blender, purée the mango cubes with the lime juice. Sweeten to taste with a little honey or agave syrup.

Whisk the cream to soft peaks and sweeten with a little more honey or agave. Place a dollop of the mango purée in the bottom of a martini glass, drop a few raspberries in, and top with a dollop of whipped cream. Repeat the mango, raspberry, and cream layers and garnish with a few more berries on top. Repeat with three additional glasses. Chill.

Prep Time: 10 minutes

SWEETHEART DINNER

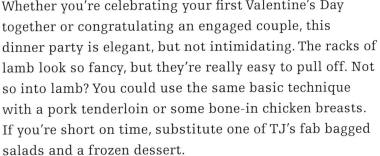

- ○ **LOVE APPLE AND BLOOD ORANGE SALAD**
- ○ **ISRAELI COUSCOUS**
- ○ **RACKS OF LAMB WITH PANKO-PISTACHIO CRUST AND DRIED CHERRY SAUCE**
- ○ **BALSAMIC-CHERRY HEARTS**
- ○ **PERSEPHONE'S DEMISE**

Whether you're celebrating your first Valentine's Day together or congratulating an engaged couple, this dinner party is elegant, but not intimidating. The racks of lamb look so fancy, but they're really easy to pull off. Not so into lamb? You could use the same basic technique with a pork tenderloin or some bone-in chicken breasts. If you're short on time, substitute one of TJ's fab bagged salads and a frozen dessert.

LOVE APPLE and BLOOD ORANGE SALAD

The tomato is said to have aphrodisiacal powers—it was once known as the love apple. Add some blood oranges to the mix, and you've got a beautiful, sexy salad. I love blood oranges, especially since their short season coincides with the dreariest days of winter. So cheering on a February dinner table!

1 (4-ounce bag) mâche lettuce or another salad mix

1 cup Trader Joe's Mixed Medley Cherry Tomatoes

1 blood orange (or regular orange), segmented (see Techniques section)

2 tablespoons Trader Joe's Orange Muscat Champagne Vinegar

1 teaspoon Dijon mustard

1/3 cup olive oil

salt and pepper

VEGAN, GLUTEN-FREE

Arrange the greens on a platter. Scatter the tomatoes and orange segments over the greens. In a small bowl, whisk together the vinegar and mustard, then slowly drizzle in the oil, whisking constantly. Season the dressing to taste with salt and pepper, and drizzle over salad.

Prep Time: 5 minutes

ISRAELI COUSCOUS

*I love Israeli couscous—such roly-poly cuteness. It lends
itself to many flavor combinations and makes a great bed
for grilled or roasted meats or fish.*

2 tablespoons butter

1 (8-ounce) box Trader Joe's
Israeli Couscous

1¾ cups chicken
(or vegetable) broth

¼ cup pitted green olives
(whole or coarsely chopped)

½ red onion, brushed with
olive oil and grilled or
pan-seared until softened and
charred, then coarsely chopped

salt and pepper

DO AHEAD
*(reheat in low oven or
microwave)*
VEGETARIAN
(if vegetable broth is used)
VEGAN
*(if vegetable broth is used and
oil is used instead of butter)*

In a medium saucepan, melt the butter and sauté the
couscous until golden, about 3 minutes. Cover the
couscous with the chicken broth and bring to a boil.
Reduce heat to low, cover, and simmer until tender, about
12 minutes. (Check to make sure there is enough liquid
to keep the couscous from sticking or burning.) When
the grains are tender, stir in the olives and chopped red
onion. Season to taste with salt and pepper.

Prep Time: 5 minutes
Cooking Time: 15 minutes

RACKS of LAMB with PANKO-PISTACHIO CRUST and DRIED CHERRY SAUCE

Even folks who profess to be lamb-haters love this. The racks are so elegant looking, they're hard to resist. The flavor of this lamb is mild, and the sauce really complements the meat.

2 (1½-pound) unseasoned frenched lamb racks (from the fresh-meat section)

1 tablespoon olive oil

about ¼ cup Dijon mustard

1 cup Trader Joe's Japanese-Style Panko Bread Crumbs

1 cup chopped pistachios

salt and pepper

DO AHEAD
(to point of roasting in oven)

Preheat oven to 425°F. Season lamb racks with salt and pepper. In a large sauté pan, heat the olive oil and brown the lamb well, 3 to 4 minutes on both sides. Spread both sides of the meat with Dijon mustard. Combine the panko and pistachios, and press the mixture firmly onto the meat. Place lamb back into the sauté pan and place in preheated oven. Bake until medium-rare (about 12 minutes), or to desired degree of doneness (2 to 3 minutes more for medium, 4 to 6 minutes more for well-done). Slice the racks between the bones into chops. Serve with Dried Cherry Sauce (page 48).

Prep Time: 15 minutes
Cooking Time: 30 minutes

• •

Trader Joe's sells frozen racks of lamb that are already seasoned. If you're pressed for time, skip the panko crust and sauce and just cook those racks according to the package directions. They're really tasty. Even quicker, TJ's carries fully seasoned and cooked heat-and-serve lamb racks! Find those near the lunch meats.

• •

DRIED CHERRY SAUCE

The rich, ruby color of the sauce is a great pairing for the racks of lamb. As a bonus, the remaining Zinfandel will be terrific to drink with the meal. Waste not, want not!

1 tablespoon unsalted butter

1 tablespoon chopped shallots

1 cube frozen garlic

2 cups beef broth

½ cup Zinfandel

1 sprig (3 to 4 inches) fresh rosemary

⅓ cup dried cherries, divided

1 to 2 tablespoons crème fraîche

salt and freshly ground black pepper

Heat the butter in a saucepan and sauté the shallots until softened, about 5 minutes. Add the garlic and sauté until fragrant, 1 to 2 minutes. Add broth, wine, and rosemary sprig, and bring to a boil. Reduce heat and simmer until reduced to about 1 cup. Add half the dried cherries and a little salt and pepper, and simmer 5 to 6 minutes. Strain the sauce, discarding the solids. Finely chop and add the remaining dried cherries and the crème fraîche to the sauce, and season to taste with salt and freshly ground black pepper.

Prep Time: 10 minutes
Cooking Time: 20 minutes

BALSAMIC-CHERRY HEARTS

These are as pretty as a specialty bakery dessert, but take hardly any time to put together.

1 (16- to 24-ounce) tea cake (Walnut Streusel, Pumpkin, Lemon, or whatever you like)

1 cup Trader Joe's Dark Morello Cherries in Light Syrup (jarred), plus ½ cup of the syrup

½ cup sugar

2 tablespoons balsamic vinegar

vanilla ice cream

dark chocolate shavings, for garnish

VEGETARIAN

Slice four 1-inch slices from the tea cake. Using a paring knife or cookie cutter, cut into heart shapes. In a sauté pan, bring the cherries, reserved cherry syrup, sugar, and balsamic vinegar to a boil. Reduce heat and simmer until syrupy, about 8 minutes. Place each heart on a serving plate, top with a scoop of ice cream, spoon some balsamic-cherry sauce on top, and garnish with dark chocolate shavings.

Prep Time: 5 minutes
Cooking Time: 10 minutes

PERSEPHONE'S DEMISE

Pomegranate's antioxidant properties have been big news recently. I guess that makes this a health-drink, right?

FOR EACH DRINK:

3 pomegranate arils

1 ounce pomegranate juice

Prosecco, or another sparkling wine

Place pomegranate arils in the bottom of a Champagne flute. Add pomegranate juice and fill flute with Prosecco or other sparkling wine.

MARDI GRAS

- **SEAFOOD SAUSAGE PO' BOYS**
- **MAQUE CHOUX CAKES**
- **BANANAS FOSTER BABY CAKES**
- **TROPICAL HURRICANE**

You don't have to wait until Lent starts to get your Mardi Gras on. Anytime you want to chase the blues away, put some Dr. John on the iPod (or go old-school with Louis Armstrong) and get into the kitchen. Pour yourself something to sip while you sauté, and before you know it, you'll feel like flingin' some beads!

SEAFOOD SAUSAGE PO' BOYS

We can't get the real-deal po' boy bread outside New Orleans, but these drippy little bundles of seafood goodness will do, until my next trip to that lovely city.

1 (12.6-ounce) package panini rolls

1 cup shredded cabbage

¼ cup organic mayonnaise

2 tablespoons red wine vinegar

1 (16-ounce) package Seafood Sausage (in the frozen fish section), thawed

2 teaspoons olive oil

1 ripe tomato, thinly sliced

salt and pepper

Split the rolls for sandwiches, leaving each one with a bread "hinge" to hold the rolls together. Toss the cabbage with mayonnaise and vinegar. Season to taste with salt and pepper. In a sauté pan, heat the oil and brown the sausages on all sides, about 6 minutes total. Split each sausage open lengthwise, and cook the cut sides a minute or two to finish cooking the fish. Place one split sausage in each roll and top with dressed cabbage and a tomato slice or two.

Prep Time: 15 minutes
Cooking Time: 10 minutes

MAQUE CHOUX CAKES

That TJ's corn salsa is definitely worth hoarding! And it has so many uses—as a taco topper, tossed into salads, stirred into soups, and mixed into brown rice. Really yummy stuff!

1 egg

4 tablespoons milk

½ cup flour

pinch baking powder

½ cup finely chopped raw shrimp

1½ cups Trader Joe's Corn and Chile Tomato-Less Salsa

pinch of salt

olive oil, for baking sheet

Preheat oven to 425°F. In a medium bowl, stir together egg and milk. Add flour and baking powder and stir to combine. The mixture will be thick. Stir in chopped shrimp and corn salsa. Add salt. Lightly oil a baking sheet and spoon dollops onto the pan, leaving 1½ inches between the cakes. Bake 10 minutes, flip with a spatula, and bake another 10 minutes. Serve immediately.

Prep Time: 5 minutes
Cooking Time: 20 minutes

These are one of the few foods I've encountered that are as good—or better—baked as they are fried. Hooray!

BANANAS FOSTER BABY CAKES

These are terrific served warm with a little vanilla ice cream, but they're also tasty at room temperature. And I hate bananas, so you know they must be good!

1½ sticks unsalted butter, at room temperature, divided

⅓ cup dark rum, divided

½ cup brown sugar

2 bananas

¾ cup milk

1 (16-ounce) box Trader Joe's Vanilla Cake and Baking Mix

2 eggs

DO AHEAD
VEGETARIAN

Preheat oven to 375°F. Line a muffin tin with paper liners. In a small saucepan, melt 4 tablespoons (½ stick) of butter with ¼ cup of rum (set the remaining 1½ tablespoons aside) and brown sugar. Bring to a boil and cook until thickened, about 4 minutes. Carefully pour mixture into the muffin cups, dividing evenly. Slice bananas and place two or three slices into each muffin cup. Melt the remaining stick of butter. Stir in the milk and the reserved rum. Add eggs and stir to combine. Stir in the cake mix and fill muffin cups ¾ full. (You may have a little batter left over. You can discard it, or butter a soufflé cup or ramekin and bake the extra batter.) Bake 15 to 17 minutes, until a toothpick inserted into the center of a cake comes out clean. Cool 10 minutes, then invert the pan onto a cookie sheet and release the baby cakes. Peel off the paper liners.

Prep Time: 15 minutes
Cooking Time: 20 minutes

TROPICAL HURRICANE

If you have some souvenir glasses from that spring break visit to Bourbon Street, here's your chance to break them out!

FOR EACH DRINK:

1 ounce light rum

1 ounce dark rum

4 ounces mango–passion fruit juice

juice of ½ a fresh lime

In a tall cocktail glass with ice, stir together all ingredients.

GRAB & GO
No-Prep Mardi Gras

Sadly, they don't sell Mardi Gras beads or boas at TJ's, but you can compensate with great grub. In New Orleans, they call grocery shopping "making groceries," and you can make some good ones at TJ's!

- **PIMENTO CHEESE**

From the frozen section:

- **SHRIMP ETOUFFÉE**
- **SEAFOOD CRAB CAKES**

RED CARPET VIEWING

- ○ **BELUGA CROSTINI**
- ○ **HARRY WINSTON JEWELED SALAD**
- ○ **BOW TIE PASTA WITH HAM**
- ○ **DROWNED ICE CREAM**

If you aren't nominated, no worries. Next year may be your year! In the meantime, gather some buddies and snark about the fashions and acceptance speeches—I'm pretty sure that's more fun than squeezing into a tux or pinchy shoes anyway.

BELUGA CROSTINI

Back in the day, Trader Joe's did carry real-deal caviar, but no more. They do, however, have the precooked packages of jet-black lentils, called beluga lentils. The black-and-white color scheme is classic, and works for a red carpet event or for watching one on TV.

¼ baguette, cut into ¼-inch rounds

½ (5.2-ounces) package Boursin Garlic and Fine Herbs Gournay cheese or goat cheese, at room temperature

2 tablespoons Black Beluga Lentils, fully cooked, (in a vacuum pack with the canned beans)

black pepper

organic microgreens, for garnish

VEGETARIAN

Toast baguette rounds, if desired. Spread with cheese and top with lentils. Grind black pepper over the top and garnish with microgreens.

Prep Time: 5 to 10 minutes

HARRY WINSTON JEWELED SALAD

Glistening jewels of pomegranate, shiny edamame, and lots of "carats," of course. The look of this salad is award-winning, and the flavor is terrific.

1 (4-ounce) bag mâche lettuce or Trader Joe's Baby Spring Mix

large handful of pomegranate arils

handful of shelled edamame

handful of shredded carrots

2 tablespoons red wine vinegar

2 teaspoons Trader Joe's Organic Blue Agave Syrup

⅓ cup olive oil

salt and pepper

VEGAN, GLUTEN-FREE

Arrange the greens on individual chilled plates. Scatter the pomegranate arils, edamame, and shredded carrots evenly over the salads. In a small bowl, whisk together the vinegar and agave syrup, and, still whisking, drizzle the oil in a little at a time, until incorporated. Season to taste with salt and pepper and drizzle over salads.

Prep Time: 5 minutes

You may have a little extra dressing—don't overdress the salad. You don't want to make anyone's worst-dressed list!

BOW TIE PASTA *with* HAM

I'll admit to being corny enough to enjoy the joke of serving farfalle—bow tie–shaped pasta—for an awards-show viewing. The flashes of color remind me of the "cause ribbons" that celebs sport on their lapels, and there's certainly plenty of ham in Hollywood. Of course, in this case, it's ham with an attitude—pancetta!

1 (16-ounce) bag farfalle, cooked al dente (reserve ½ cup pasta water)

1 tablespoon olive oil

1 (4-ounce) package cubed pancetta

1 pint Trader Joe's Minisweet Bell Peppers, cut into strips

½ cup dry white wine

salt, pepper, and grated Parmesan cheese

Cook the pasta and reserve ½ cup of the cooking water. In a sauté pan, heat the olive oil and brown the pancetta, 3 to 4 minutes. Add the mini-pepper strips and sauté until tender, 3 to 4 minutes. Add the wine and simmer 2 to 3 minutes. Toss pasta with pepper mixture. Add the reserved pasta water if you like the pasta saucier. Add a little Parmesan cheese, toss, and adjust seasoning to taste with salt, pepper, and additional Parmesan.

Prep Time: 10 minutes
Cooking Time: 15 minutes

Be sure to add some of the Parmesan before you salt the pasta. The Parm is salty on its own, and you don't want to oversalt the dish.

DROWNED ICE CREAM

In Hollywood, everyone has their own espresso maker, and no one really eats dessert. If you don't have an in-home barista, and you do eat dessert, you can use strong coffee or choose limoncello or Kahlúa to drown your ice cream.

FOR EACH SERVING:
1 scoop vanilla ice cream
splash of espresso
1 Cocoa Meringue

VEGETARIAN

Scoop the ice cream into a dish and pour the espresso over the ice cream. Crumble the meringue over the top.

Prep Time: 5 minutes

The hot liquid will melt the ice cream into a soupy, coffee-flavored treat. The meringue adds texture—a crunchy counterpoint to the creamy goodness.

GRAB & GO
Red Carpet Champagne

"Come quickly! I'm drinking stars"—that's what Dom Perignon reportedly exclaimed when he first tasted the happy accident that became the most elegant sipper of all, champagne. One lucky monk he was! I love the mystique, the look, the tickle, and, of course, the toasty taste of sparkling wine. In order to properly be called Champagne, the bubbly must be made in the Champagne region of northern France. But great sparkling wine? That can come from lots of less-pedigreed real estate. In Spain, there's Cava, and Italy produces Prosecco. And let's not leave out California!

TJ's carries a shelf-full of wire-topped bottles of all origins. One of my faves is Piper Sonoma—at about $12, it's a great bargain, and I love its pinpoint starburst bubbles. (I've heard that the smaller the bubbles, the smaller the hangover, so beware those big "toad's eye" buoys in the cheap stuff!) When I graduated from culinary school, I was gifted with some terrific (and pricey) bottles of bubbles, so we decided to throw a party and do a blind tasting. While the Piper was not everyone's number one, it did win as the overall favorite, much to a thoroughly French chef's dismay! You'll find several champagne-based cocktails in the book; but as for me, on red carpet evenings, I'll take my sparklers unadorned.

RAINY NIGHT IN

- **DRIZZLY DAY SALAD**
- **CROQUE MONSIEUR (FRENCH GRILLED CHEESE)**
- **GREEN CHILE-CORN SOUP**
- **MEDIA NOCHE**
- **DARK AND STORMY (WHAT ELSE?)**
- **MEXICAN CHOCOLATE BREAD PUDDING**

No need to be gloomy, even if that's the forecast. Maybe it's you and the kids, curling up with a movie or Jenga, maybe it's the neighbors and a bottle of wine? Snuggle in with some soup and listen to the rain on the roof. Cozy good times!

DRIZZLY DAY SALAD

I love the crispy hearts of butter lettuce in this salad mix, along with the slightly bitter, vivid red radicchio. Add the crunch of pecans, the sweetness of cranberries, and a salty bite of blue cheese, and I'm a happy girl! Toss some crisp bacon bits in, if you like. It's a winning combo, with or without the pork.

1 (7-ounce) bag Trader Joe's Butter Lettuce and Radicchio

handful of shredded carrots

1 ripe avocado, sliced

½ (5-ounce) bag Trader Joe's Rosemary Pecans and Cranberries

¼ cup crumbled blue cheese

1 teaspoons Dijon mustard

2 tablespoons red wine vinegar

⅓ cup olive oil

salt and pepper

VEGETARIAN

In a salad bowl, toss together the lettuce, carrots, avocado slices, and pecans and cranberries. In a small bowl, whisk together the crumbled blue cheese, mustard, vinegar, and olive oil to make a chunky dressing. Season with salt and pepper and dress the salad.

Prep Time: 5 minutes

CROQUE MONSIEUR (FRENCH GRILLED CHEESE)

I only have these once or twice a year, but I look forward to them the rest of the time! So ooey-gooey-good, they're worth the time it takes to make them.

5 tablespoons butter, divided

4 tablespoons flour

¾ cup milk

1 teaspoon Dijon mustard

1 egg yolk, slightly beaten

nutmeg, salt, and white pepper

8 slices good-quality white bread

1 cup grated Gruyère cheese

4 slices good-quality ham (Black Forest or Rosemary Ham)

VEGETARIAN *(omit the ham)*

In a small saucepan, melt 4 tablespoons of the butter (reserving 1 tablespoon) and whisk in the flour. Cook 2 to 3 minutes, until the mixture is smooth and smells nutty. Add the milk and bring to a boil. Reduce heat and simmer until thickened, about 4 minutes. Stir in mustard. Add about one quarter of the hot milk mixture to the egg yolk, stirring as you add. When the mixture is well blended, return it to the remainder of the hot milk. Season to taste with salt, white pepper, and a little nutmeg.

Butter one side of each piece of bread, using the remaining 1 tablespoon of butter. Place the slices, butter side down, on a work surface, and spread the plain side of each piece of bread with about a tablespoon of the béchamel (white sauce). Sprinkle about 2 tablespoons of the grated cheese on half the bread slices. (Reserve a little cheese for the tops of the sandwiches.) Top the cheese with a slice of ham, then top with one of the remaining bread slices with the buttered side out. Heat a sauté pan and brown the sandwiches on each side. Preheat the broiler, spread a little béchamel on the top of each sandwich, and sprinkle with the remaining cheese. Place the sandwiches under the broiler for a moment, watching carefully, until the tops are browned and bubbly.

Prep Time: 15 minutes
Cooking Time: 20 minutes

GREEN CHILE-CORN SOUP

Here's a creamy, spicy, smoky bowl of comfort that's quick to put together and makes the house smell terrific!

3 strips Niman Ranch Applewood Smoked Dry-Cured Bacon

1 (4-ounce) package chopped onion, shallot, and garlic

1 tablespoon flour

2 (4-ounce) cans Hatch Valley Fire-Roasted Diced Green Chiles

1 cup chicken broth

½ cup cream

½ bag frozen roasted corn

about ½ cup grated cheddar cheese, or other cheese blend (optional)

DO AHEAD

In a medium saucepan, cook the bacon until crisp. Remove the strips and reserve. In the same pan, sauté the chopped onion, shallot, and garlic in the bacon drippings until softened and fragrant. Add the flour and cook 2 to 3 minutes. Add the chiles and chicken broth and bring to a boil. Reduce heat and simmer 5 minutes. Add the cream and corn and simmer until corn is warmed, about 3 minutes. Season to taste with salt and pepper, and stir in grated cheese, if using. Crumble the cooked bacon over the soup for garnish.

Prep Time: 10 minutes
Cooking Time: 30 minutes

MEDIA NOCHE

These may not be strictly authentic, but if you don't live near a Cuban bakery, they'll do! I love the crunch of the grilled bread, the briny snap of the pickle, and the sweet-salty goodness of the ham. Use turkey if you like, instead of—or in addition to—the pork.

1 (12.6-ounce) package
panini rolls

about 2 tablespoons
Trader Joe's Deli Style Spicy
Brown Mustard

about 2 tablespoons organic
mayonnaise

4 slices Swiss or Havarti cheese

4 pickle strips

4 slices Black Forest Healthy
Smoked Ham

melted butter

Heat a griddle, grill pan, or a panini maker. Split each roll lengthwise and spread lightly with mustard and mayonnaise. Place the cheese on one side of the bread and the pickle slices on the other side. Layer the meat on top of the pickles and close the sandwich. Brush both sides of each roll with a little melted butter and grill the sandwiches on each side, pressing down firmly or weighting, until crisp and flattened.

Prep Time: 10 minutes
Cooking Time: 5 minutes per sandwich

DARK AND STORMY

Drink what you like—I couldn't resist pairing this beverage with the theme. But if it's too cold for Dark and Stormies, try TJ's terrific cocoa (or seasonally available Sipping Chocolate) with a shot of Drambuie or Frangelico—for the adults, of course. That'll warm you right up.

FOR EACH DRINK:
¾ cup Reed's
Extra Ginger Brew
Ginger Beer

¼ cup Whaler's Dark Rum

ice

Place a few ice cubes in a cocktail glass. Add the ginger beer to the glass and top with the rum.

MEXICAN CHOCOLATE BREAD PUDDING

Desserts don't get homier or more snuggle-worthy than bread pudding. A dollop of vanilla ice cream would put this over the top...the creamy coolness melting into the hot, fragrant, chocolatey bread pudding? Heaven!

about 2 tablespoons melted butter and sugar, for ramekins

1 cup half-and-half

3 ounces bittersweet chocolate, coarsely chopped (see note)

zest of 1 orange

pinch of salt

1 teaspoon vanilla

1 tablespoons Kahlúa

4 eggs

¼ cup brown sugar

3 cups cubed brioche or other white bread (crusts removed, cut into ½-inch cubes)

DO AHEAD
VEGETARIAN

Preheat oven to 375°F. Butter four ramekins and shake sugar around each one to coat sides. In a saucepan, heat the half-and-half to a boil. Place chopped chocolate and orange zest in a large bowl and pour in the hot half-and-half. Let stand about 5 minutes, then stir to combine. Stir in the salt, vanilla, and Kalhúa. In a separate bowl, whisk together the eggs and brown sugar, and add to the chocolate mixture. Add the bread cubes and let stand 15 minutes, stirring several times to incorporate. Fill the ramekins evenly with the bread and custard mixture. Place the ramekins on a baking sheet (to contain any spills) and bake until set and puffed, about 25 minutes. Cool slightly before serving.

Prep Time: 25 minutes
Cooking Time: 25 minutes

• •
TJ's is well-stocked with many good chocolate bars. Try their Organic Dark Chocolate, Fair Trade Swiss Dark Chocolate, or the Valrhona 71% Le Noir Amer. They all come in 3.5-ounce bars, which means there's an extra half-ounce for the cook to nibble on!
• •

ST. PATRICK'S DAY

- CRAB CORACLES
- CHEESY CHAMP
- CIDER-GLAZED CORNED BEEF AND CABBAGE
- GUINNESS AND COFFEE CUPCAKES
- BLACK VELVET

I'm not sure if St. Paddy's Day is as celebrated in Ireland as it is in the States—but when cities dye their rivers to celebrate, that's some serious commitment to the wearin' of the green. If you aren't into corned beef, this recipe might change your mind. Of course, you could always go with salmon or lamb for another Erin-appropriate entrée.

CRAB CORACLES

A coracle is an Irish (or Welsh) rowboat. With a little imagination, these sweet, crabby morsels look a little like the tiny seaworthy vessels. Or maybe that's the Guinness talking? Anyway, they're as delicious as they are cute.

1 (9-ounce) bag snow peas

½ (16-ounce) can refrigerated crabmeat

½ cup minced celery

1 tablespoon capers, chopped

2 tablespoons mayonnaise

2 tablespoons Trader Joe's Aioli Garlic Mustard Sauce

salt and pepper

DO AHEAD

Fill a medium bowl with ice cubes and cold water. Bring a pot of salted water to a boil. Blanch the snow peas just until tender, about 30 seconds, and remove to the ice bath to stop the cooking process and set the peas' bright green color. Drain and pat dry. Split the peas open along the top edges. Combine the crabmeat, celery, capers, mayonnaise, and aioli sauce, and season to taste with salt and pepper. Stuff each snow pea with about a teaspoonful of the crab mixture. Chill until ready to serve.

Prep Time: 15 minutes
Cooking Time: 30 seconds

Use the extra crabmeat to form crabcakes—so, so good coated in TJ's super-crispy panko crumbs and pan-fried in a little butter. I love a couple on top of salad greens.

CHEESY CHAMP

Champ is an Irish mashed potato dish flavored with green onions (aka scallions). I've added some Dubliner, a great Irish cheese, because...well, because then it's a potato and cheese dish, and what could be better than that? Hmmm... maybe a potato, cheese, and bacon dish! Add some crisp, crumbled bacon to this, and I'll be right over! Leftovers—with or without the bacon—thinned with vegetable or chicken stock make a terrific soup the next day.

1 pound russet potatoes, peeled and cut into 1½-inch cubes

5 green onions, thinly sliced

3 tablespoons butter

1 cup grated Dubliner cheese

salt and pepper

DO AHEAD
(reheat in low oven or microwave)
VEGETARIAN

Place the potato cubes in a large saucepan and cover with cold water. Bring to a boil and cook until potatoes are tender, 12 to 15 minutes. Place the green onions in the bottom of a colander. Reserve about a cup of the cooking water before draining potatoes. Drain potatoes through the colander. Return potatoes and green onions to the pan and shake them around a bit. (The hot pan will help dry the surface of the potatoes a little bit, which will make them easier to mash.) Use a potato masher or wooden spoon to mash up the potatoes. Add the butter and cheese, and stir to combine. Add a little of the reserved potato water and stir. Continue adding potato water until you achieve the desired consistency. (The texture will be "rustic"—on the chunky side, rather than creamy.) Season with salt and pepper.

Prep Time: 10 minutes
Cooking Time: 20 minutes

Putting the green onions in the colander before you drain the potatoes softens them a little bit when the hot potato water wilts them. (Crunchy mashed potatoes would be a little strange, no?) If you want a variation, use a bag of TJ's shredded cabbage instead of the onions. Use the same wilting method and stir into the potatoes. This dish is known as colcannon.

CIDER-GLAZED CORNED BEEF and CABBAGE

The sweetness of the cider pairs so well with the earthiness of the salted beef and braised vegetables. This may not be a strictly traditional preparation, but it's strictly delicious.

1 (2- to 3-pound) package uncured corned beef

1 (22-ounce) bottle Ace pear cider

1 head baby cabbage, cut into six wedges

½ (16-ounce) bag cut and peeled baby carrots

1 pound red potatoes, quartered, (optional)

freshly ground black pepper

GLUTEN-FREE

Preheat oven to 325°F. Place the beef in a Dutch oven (or other stovetop and ovenproof pot with lid) and pour cider over it. If there isn't enough cider to almost cover the meat, add more cider or water. Bring to a boil, cover, and place pot in oven. Cook 2 hours. Add cabbage wedges, carrots, and potato quarters (if using), and spoon some of the cooking liquid over them. Cover and return pot to the oven for another hour. Test to see if meat and vegetables are fork-tender. If not, return to oven for another 30 to 45 minutes. When the meat and vegetables are tender, slice the meat and arrange meat and vegetables on a serving platter. Return the pot to the stovetop. Boil the cooking liquid until thickened, about 8 minutes, and spoon over meat and vegetables. Season with black pepper.

Prep Time: 5 minutes
Cooking Time: 3½ hours

GUINNESS *and* COFFEE CUPCAKES

Beer cupcakes? Why not? Well, technically, Guinness isn't beer—it's an Irish stout, a style of brewing that results in that distinctively dark color and toasty, almost coffeelike flavors. Cakes containing Guinness have gained popularity in recent years, thanks in part to Nigella Lawson, the British kitchen goddess. The cream-cheesy frosting brings to mind that foamy Guinness head.

CUPCAKES:

½ cup Guinness

½ cup (1 stick) butter

1 (16-ounce) box Trader Joe's Brownie Truffle Baking Mix

2 eggs

FROSTING:

1 (8-ounce) container mascarpone

4 tablespoons butter, at room temperature

1 tablespoon brewed coffee (or 1 teaspoon instant coffee granules)

1½ to 2 cups powdered sugar

DO AHEAD
VEGETARIAN

FOR CUPCAKES: Preheat oven to 350°F. Line a muffin tin with paper liners. In a medium saucepan, bring the Guinness and butter to a boil. Reduce heat and simmer until the butter is melted. Add baking mix and stir to combine. Crack the eggs into a small bowl and whisk to combine. Stir eggs into Guinness mixture. Fill paper liners ⅔ full. Bake until a toothpick inserted into the center of a cupcake comes out clean, about 25 minutes. Cool before frosting.

FOR FROSTING: With an electric mixer, combine the mascarpone, butter, and coffee. Beat in 1½ cups powdered sugar. Adjust sweetness to taste with additional powdered sugar, if desired. Frost the cooled cupcakes.

Prep Time: 20 minutes
Cooking Time: 25 minutes

Powdered sugar is a seasonal item at Trader Joe's, so stock up, or use some from (gasp!) another store.

BLACK VELVET

This simple sipper was supposedly created while Britain mourned the death of Queen Victoria's beloved Prince Albert.

Guinness
champagne

For each drink, fill a champagne flute halfway with Guinness. Carefully pour an equal amount of champagne over the back of a spoon, on top of the Guinness. The spoon helps the two liquids to form separate layers in the glass.

WINE TASTING PARTY

- SMOKED SALMON QUICHE
- SAVORY CHEESE CRISPS
- PORK MEDALLIONS WITH ROSEMARY AND MUSHROOMS
- HEART OF DARKNESS CHOCOLATE TORTE

We love to invite friends over for wine tasting. We usually set a theme—TJ's Wine Finds, ABC (Anything But Chardonnay), Great Deal Reds, Rhone Varietals, or Rockin' Rosés—and have everybody bring a bottle. Then we bag them up, so no one knows whose is whose, and start pouring. I'm a firm believer in trying all the wines without food, first. (OK, Maria—you can have water crackers...I know you need *something*!) Then sip again with food, and see how it changes the flavors! It makes for such a fun evening, and we usually end up with a couple new favorites!

SMOKED SALMON QUICHE

This is rich, so serve little squares or skinny slivers as a first course. It's a great lunch on top of greens and vinaigrette, too.

1 Trader Joe's Gourmet Pie Crust (in the frozen-food section), defrosted (refreeze the remaining one for another use)

1 tablespoon butter

1 shallot, chopped

3 eggs

1½ cups cream

zest of 1 lemon

4 ounces smoked salmon, chopped

4 ounces goat cheese, crumbled

2 tablespoons capers

salt and pepper

DO AHEAD

Preheat oven to 350°F. Blind-bake the pie dough (see Techniques section). Cool to room temperature. In a small sauté pan, melt the butter and sauté the shallot until tender and fragrant, about 4 minutes. Cool to room temperature. Whisk together the eggs and cream. Add lemon zest, chopped salmon, goat cheese, sautéed shallots, and capers. Season lightly with salt and pepper. Pour into pastry shell and bake until center is just set, about 30 minutes. Cool 15 minutes before slicing.

Prep Time: 15 minutes
Cooking Time: 35 minutes

The richness of the salmon pairs beautifully with bubbles, so pop the cork on a Cava, Prosecco, Champagne, or another sparkler.

SAVORY CHEESE CRISPS

TJ's recently introduced three new grated cheese blends—I can't decide which is my favorite. One is a Gruyère and Swiss blend, another is Spicy Jack with other spicy cheeses, and the third is a smoky blend. You can use any of them in these crazy-good crisps.

4 ounces butter,
at room temperature

2 cups grated cheese
(like the Trader Joe's Smoked
or Pepper Jack Shredded
Cheese Blends)

1 cup flour

pinch of salt

VEGETARIAN

With a mixer, combine the butter and cheese. Add the flour and salt, and mix just until combined. Transfer onto a sheet of parchment and form into a log, about 10 inches long and 1½ inches in diameter. Refrigerate at least 30 minutes. Preheat oven to 350°F. Slice ¼-inch thick rounds from the log and place on a parchment-lined baking sheet. Bake until golden, 15 to 18 minutes.

Prep Time: 5 minutes, plus 30 minutes chilling time
Cooking Time: under 20 minutes

Great with Chardonnay. Serve with a cheese platter, along with grapes and seasonal fruit, water crackers, and some almonds.

PORK MEDALLIONS *with* ROSEMARY *and* MUSHROOMS

Deep, foresty flavors for rich reds. This is one of my favorite ways to cook pork. Pan-searing the medallions creates lots of brown goodness—called "fond"—on the bottom of the pan. Deglazing with vermouth or wine will bring that flavorful stuff right into your sauce.

1½ to 1¾ pounds pork tenderloin, cut into ¾-inch medallions

1 tablespoon olive oil

2 cubes frozen garlic

1 tablespoon chopped fresh rosemary

salt and pepper

1½ cups sliced mushrooms (crimini, portobello, shiitake, or a combination)

1 cup vermouth or red wine

½ (8-ounce) container crème fraîche

Season pork medallions with salt and pepper. Heat oil in a sauté pan and, working in batches, sear all the medallions on both sides, about 3 minutes per side. As meat is seared, remove to a platter. When all pork is seared, sauté garlic and rosemary until fragrant, 1 to 2 minutes. Add mushrooms and sauté until tender, about 6 minutes. Carefully add vermouth or wine, bring to a boil, and reduce heat. Simmer until reduced by half, 5 to 6 minutes. Add crème fraîche and warm through. Add pork medallions and any accumulated juices to sauce, and simmer until pork is cooked through. (This will take a few minutes, depending on how browned the medallions are.) Adjust seasoning to taste with salt and pepper.

Prep Time: 15 minutes
Cooking Time: 30 minutes

The TJ's Organic Polenta in a tube is a great accompaniment for this dish. Slice, brown in a little olive oil or butter, and use as a bed for the pork and mushroom sauce. Mashed potatoes or rice work, too. Pour a lush Zinfandel or Syrah—try Jepson, or Trader Joe's Reserve Syrah. So good, for so little!

HEART OF DARKNESS CHOCOLATE TORTE

Serious stuff here. Dense and almost pure chocolate, this torte should be served in slivers. Oh, boy—that means leftovers! Remember, research shows that dark chocolate and red wine are good for us. My favorite antioxidants!

1 (17.6-ounce) Trader Joe's Pound Plus Bittersweet Chocolate bar, chopped

8 ounces butter, at room temperature

¼ cup Trader Joe's Just Almond Meal

4 eggs, separated

¼ cup sugar

1 pint fresh raspberries

DO AHEAD
VEGETARIAN, GLUTEN-FREE

Preheat oven to 400°F. Butter an 8-inch removable-bottom cake pan or springform pan. In a double boiler, melt the chocolate. When chocolate is smooth and melted, whisk in butter until melted. Whisk in almond meal. In a separate bowl, whisk together the egg yolks and sugar, then whisk into chocolate mixture. Cool to room temperature. Beat egg whites to soft peaks and fold into the chocolate mixture. Gently fold in raspberries. Spoon batter into prepared pan. Bake 25 minutes. Turn oven off and allow cake to cool in oven, with the door ajar, 1 hour. Refrigerate overnight. Use a paring knife to release sides of torte from cake pan and unmold. Cut into thin slices for serving.

Prep Time: 30 minutes
Cooking Time: 25 minutes, plus overnight chilling

• •

This is gorgeous on its own, but if you feel the need to garnish, resist whipped cream. It's too frou-frou for this. Go with a few raspberries, a dusting of powdered sugar, or barely sweetened, whipped crème fraîche.

• •

GRAB & GO
Wine Tasting, TJ's Style

Trader Joe's got its start bringing little-known, great-value wines to market. In fact, California makers owe a big thank you to Joe Coloumbe and his team, as they really helped popularize the state's burgeoning wine industry back in the day. TJ's continues to do a great job searching out value-priced, well-crafted wines, as well as unbelievably low-priced sippers like Charles Shaw— better known as "Two [or Three, depending on the state] Buck Chuck." Most TJ's stores have a wine expert or two (great job, huh?) who are more than happy to guide, suggest, and personally recommend wines for your palate and pocketbook. Watch for "hustle buys"—particularly tasty stuff that TJ's has purchased the entire run of. These are "going, going, gone" items, so if you find one you love, grab more quick! I enjoy several of their Jepson varietals—Sauvignon Blanc and Syrah—as well as the Trader Joe's Grower's Reserves. There is an online cultlike following for the Chariot Gypsy blend that's released each year—people plan road trips to stock up when it shows up on the TJ's shelves!

SPRING FLING

- **PAPPARDELLE WITH SUGAR SNAP PEAS AND PANCETTA**
- **GRILLED ASPARAGUS WITH CHEATER'S SAFFRON AIOLI**
- **WASABI SALMON**
- **BOUNTIFUL BERRY TART**
- **MARCH MOJITOS**

When the leaf buds start to unfurl and the air is a little warmer on our skin, our bodies tend to crave lighter, cleaner flavors. Those carb-laden dinners, so comforting in cold weather, seem too stodgy for spring. Spring food is like spring dresses—pretty, floaty, and bright.

PAPPARDELLE *with* SUGAR SNAP PEAS *and* PANCETTA

This dish makes me ridiculously happy. I just love the look of the yellow tangle of noodles with the bright green pea pods peeking through. It looks like spring on a plate, and tastes wonderful, too.

1 (12-ounce) bag sugar snap peas

1 (4-ounce) package Trader Joe's Lemon Pepper Pappardelle pasta

2 tablespoons olive oil

1 (4-ounce) package cubed Italian-Style Bacon Pancetta

1 (.34-ounce) tube chicken broth concentrate

½ cup reserved pasta water

zest and juice of 1 lemon

½ cup frozen peas, optional

salt and pepper

shaved Toscano Cheese with Black Pepper, for garnish

Bring a medium saucepan of salted water to a boil. Place a steamer basket on top and steam the sugar snap peas just until tender, about 4 minutes. Remove steamer basket. Cook the pasta in the same water and drain, reserving about ½ cup of the pasta water.

In the same saucepan, heat the olive oil and sauté the pancetta until browned, 3 to 4 minutes. Add the broth concentrate, reserved pasta water, lemon zest and juice, and the frozen peas (if using). Simmer 1 to 2 minutes, until peas are defrosted. Add the cooked pasta and sugar snap peas to the saucepan and toss to combine. Season to taste with salt and pepper. Arrange on a platter or on individual plates, and garnish with shaved Toscano cheese.

Prep Time: 10 minutes
Cooking Time: 20 minutes

GRILLED ASPARAGUS *with* CHEATER'S SAFFRON AIOLI

If the weather is grill friendly, dust the spider webs off the barbecue and start the season off with these glorious green grillers. If it's not quite time for outdoor cooking, you can roast the asparagus in a 450°F oven for 8 to 10 minutes. You won't get the pretty grill marks, but you will get great flavor! Either way you cook them, a handful of mushrooms tossed in are terrific, too.

1 (12-ounce) package fresh asparagus spears

about 2 teaspoons olive oil

salt and pepper

VEGETARIAN, GLUTEN-FREE

Heat grill to high. Trim tough ends of asparagus and toss spears with olive oil. Season with salt and pepper and grill just until tender and a little charred, 3 to 5 minutes. Dip into Cheater's Saffron Aioli.

CHEATER'S SAFFRON AIOLI

The color of this dip is pure springtime. Saffron is super labor-intensive to produce, so it's usually uber-expensive. Once again, it's Joe's to the rescue. They sell an adorable glass bottle of great-quality saffron for about five bucks. A little goes a long way, thank goodness, so that cute little cork-stoppered vial will make a buncha batches of this lovely stuff. This dip is also great with artichokes or slathered on a sandwich!

pinch of saffron threads

juice of ½ lemon

1 cup organic mayonnaise

2 cubes frozen garlic

1 tablespoon olive oil

2 teaspoons Dijon mustard, optional

VEGETARIAN, GLUTEN-FREE

Crush the saffron threads with a mortar and pestle. Add the lemon juice and let stand 5 minutes to "melt" the saffron. Whisk together the mayonnaise, garlic, olive oil, mustard (if using), and the saffron-infused lemon juice.

Prep Time: 5 minutes
Cooking Time: 5 minutes

WASABI SALMON

Couldn't be simpler, but the flavor is great. Mayo on fish is an old grilling trick—it keeps the fish from sticking to the grates and it adds moisture and flavor. But in this recipe it works in the oven, too!

2 pounds fresh or frozen and thawed wild-caught salmon

¼ cup Trader Joe's Wasabi Mayonnaise

salt and pepper

GLUTEN-FREE

Preheat oven to 425°F. Place the salmon on a parchment-lined baking sheet. Season lightly with salt and pepper, and slather with wasabi mayonnaise. Bake 8 to 10 minutes, until fish is warm in the center. Remove to platter to serve.

Prep Time: 5 minutes
Cooking Time: 10 minutes

Here's a cheffy trick—to tell when the fish is done, insert a thin-bladed paring knife at an angle into the fish, so that about ½ inch of the blade's tip is dead-center in the middle of the fish. Hold the knife blade there for about 3 seconds, and then touch the blade tip to the skin below your lower lip. If the fish was hot enough in the center to warm the knife tip so that sensitive skin feels the heat, the fish is done.

BOUNTIFUL BERRY TART

You'll be incredibly pleased with yourself when you make this. Hundreds of cooking school students have called, written, or come back to tell me how they wow their guests with this gorgeous thing. Looks like it came right out of a pink pastry box, but so easy to do!

1 Trader Joe's Gourmet Pie Crust (in the frozen-food section), defrosted (reserve the remaining crust for another use)

¼ cup Trader Joe's Fresh Raspberry Preserves (optional)

1 (10.5-ounce) jar Trader Joe's Lemon Curd

1 (8-ounce) container mascarpone, at room temperature

2 cups berries (raspberries, blueberries, blackberries, and/or sliced strawberries)

DO AHEAD
VEGETARIAN

Preheat oven to 375°F. Roll out pie dough and fit into a 8- or 9-inch pie pan or removable-bottom tart pan. Cover the pastry with parchment paper (see note) and weight it down with pie weights, raw rice, or dry beans. Place in oven for 12 minutes. Carefully remove parchment and weight, and return pan to the oven for 5 to 10 minutes, until pastry is dry and golden. Cool to room temperature. Spread the raspberry preserves over the bottom of the crust (if using). Stir together the lemon curd and mascarpone and fill tart shell with the mixture. Arrange the berries over the tart. Chill at least 2 hours before slicing.

Prep Time: 10 minutes
Cooking Time: 25 minutes

• •
The raspberry jam does two things—it adds a double dose of berry flavor (duh!), and it also forms a bit of a moisture barrier between the crisp crust and the gooey-good lemon filling. If you're making this a day ahead, that jammy layer will help the crust from getting too soft on you.
• •
Baker's trick: Crumpling the sheet of parchment into a ball and then opening it up again will help it lay flatter inside the pan. The wrinkled paper has more "give" to it than a fresh, flat sheet, so it will conform to the interior of the pan more easily.
• •

MARCH MOJITOS

One of the first signs of spring in the garden is the vivid green of mint sprigs popping up in forgotten corners. The mint smells amazing as I brush past it and makes me crave mojitos!

FOR EACH DRINK:
8 fresh mint leaves
1½ teaspoons sugar
juice of ½ a lime
¼ cup white rum
sparkling water
ice cubes

Place the mint leaves in a cocktail glass. Add the sugar and lime juice. With a muddler or wooden spoon, mash the mint with the sugar to release as much of the oil inside the leaves as possible. Add the rum and a few ice cubes. Top off with sparkling water.

CINCO DE MAYO

- CARNITAS QUESADILLAS WITH CILANTRO ROASTED PECAN DIP
- CALABACITAS TRADER JOSÉ
- TJ TORTILLA SOUP
- ANTIOXI-GUAC
- MARGARITA TART
- POMEGRANARITA

Cinco de Mayo is big in Southern California. The weather is usually perfect for margaritas, and even if it drizzles, we can still party Mexican-style in honor of their victorious defeat of the French at the Battle of Puebla. (Even if you didn't know that's what you were celebrating, I raise my margarita glass to you!)

CARNITAS QUESADILLAS with CILANTRO ROASTED PECAN DIP

These are splurge-worthy quesadillas. Adding the Cilantro Roasted Pecan Dip to the traditional cheesy goodness lends a tang that melds beautifully with the rich flavor of the carnitas.

1 package Handmade Corn Tortillas (you'll need 8)

1 (7-ounce) container Trader Joe's Cilantro Roasted Pecan Dip

1 (12-ounce) package Trader José's Traditional Carnitas, shredded

1 cup shredded cheese blend (I love the Trader Joe's Pepper Jack Shredded Cheese Blend or Fancy Shredded Mexican Blend)

1 tablespoon grapeseed or canola oil

Start with two tortillas. Spread a couple teaspoons of cilantro dip on one side of each tortilla. Shred about 3 tablespoons of carnitas and scatter on top of one of the tortillas. Scatter about ¼ cup of the cheese on top of the carnitas. Top with the second tortilla, cilantro dip–side down. Repeat with remaining ingredients until you have assembled four quesadillas. Heat the oil in a medium sauté pan, and carefully place one quesadilla into the oil. Cook over medium heat until bottom side is golden and just crispy, about 4 minutes. With a spatula, carefully flip the quesadilla and cook about 3 minutes on the second side. Remove to a paper towel and let cool slightly before cutting into quarters. Repeat with the remaining quesadillas.

Prep Time: 15 minutes
Cooking Time: 15 minutes

CALABACITAS TRADER JOSÉ

Calabacitas *means "little squashes," and this dish has those and so much more. The zip of chiles and the pop of cherry tomatoes make this a vibrantly flavored side dish, and it looks like a fiesta on a platter.*

2 tablespoons olive oil

1 red onion, sliced

2 cubes frozen garlic

2 zucchini, sliced

2 yellow squash, sliced

1 (16-ounce) bag frozen roasted corn

1 (4-ounce) can chopped Hatch Valley Fire-Roasted Diced Green Chiles

handful of Trader Joe's Mixed Medley Cherry Tomatoes or Mini Heirloom Tomatoes

1½ cups shredded cheese (Trader Joe's Pepper Jack Shredded Cheese Blend or Fancy Shredded Mexican Blend are great for this), divided

salt and pepper

DO AHEAD
VEGETARIAN, GLUTEN-FREE

In a large sauté pan, heat the oil and sauté the red onion until softened, about 4 minutes. Add the garlic and sauté until fragrant, 1 to 2 minutes. Add the sliced zucchini and yellow squash, and sauté 3 to 4 minutes. Add the corn and sauté 3 to 4 minutes. Add the chiles and tomatoes, and sauté until warmed through. Season to taste with salt and pepper, and add 1 cup of cheese. Stir to combine, place in serving dish, and top with additional cheese.

Prep Time: 10 minutes
Cooking Time: 15 minutes

•••
Try this folded into a tortilla!
•••

TJ TORTILLA SOUP

Don't be put off by the length of the ingredient list. This soup comes together really quickly but tastes as though you simmered it for hours. It's a bowlful of fiesta flavors you'll make over and over.

1 tablespoon grapeseed or canola oil

1 cup chopped onion

1 teaspoon ground cumin

1 tablespoon Trader Joe's Taco Seasoning Mix

6 cups chicken broth

1 (15-ounce) can diced tomatoes in juice

1 (15-ounce) can kidney beans, drained and rinsed

1 (15-ounce) can black beans, drained and rinsed

1 cup shredded carrots

1 (4-ounce) can Hatch Valley Fire-Roasted Diced Green Chiles

3 ribs celery, sliced ¼-inch thick

1 (12-ounce) package Trader Joe's Just Grilled Chicken Strips, chopped

salt and pepper

TORTILLA STRIPS:

4 corn tortillas, cut in ¼-inch strips

3 tablespoons grapeseed or canola oil

Trader Joe's Taco Seasoning Mix

GLUTEN-FREE
(if gluten-free tortillas are used)

In a stockpot, heat oil and sauté onion until barely tender, about 5 minutes. Add cumin and taco seasoning and cook until fragrant, about 2 minutes. Add broth and tomatoes and bring to a boil. Lower heat, add kidney beans, black beans, carrots, green chiles, and celery, and simmer 10 minutes. Add chopped chicken and warm through. Adjust seasoning with salt, pepper, and more taco seasoning, if desired.

FOR TORTILLA STRIPS: While soup simmers, fry the tortilla strips in batches. Heat the oil in a shallow skillet, and carefully add about a quarter of the strips. Turn them with tongs, and cook until golden and crisp. Remove to layers of paper towels, and while still hot, season with taco seasoning mix.

Prep Time: 10 minutes
Cooking Time: 30 minutes

Go garnish crazy! Set out bowls of chopped cilantro, grated cheese, crème fraîche or sour cream, avocado slices, and extra tortilla strips, and let your gang customize their soup experience.

ANTIOXI-GUAC

I like my guacamole a little on the chunky side, so I don't mash the avocados too smoothly, and I add crunchy veggies. They increase nutrition and add great texture!

3 ripe avocados, peeled and cubed

¼ to ½ cup finely chopped red onion

2 green onions, chopped

juice of 1 to 2 limes

salt, pepper, and Trader Joe's Chili Pepper Hot Sauce or Jalapeño Pepper Hot Sauce

handful of pomegranate arils

DO AHEAD
VEGAN, GLUTEN-FREE

In a large bowl, mash the avocados with a fork. Stir in the chopped red and green onions and season to taste with lime juice, salt, pepper, and hot sauce. Just before serving, gently fold in the pomegranate arils, using a few to garnish the top of the guacamole.

Prep Time: 10 minutes

· ·

While untraditional in guacamole, pomegranate arils are used in Mexican cuisine. Remember, avocados contain fat, the "good" kind of fat, so if you use carrot sticks rather than fried chips in this dip, it's practically a multivitamin in a bowl.

· ·

MARGARITA TART

For a similar flavor to this tart, but with less labor, dip TJ's Lime Fruit Floe pops into tequila and sprinkling them with salt and cayenne. Note: At TJ's, sweetened condensed milk is seasonal.

CRUST:

2 cups Triple Ginger Snaps crumbs

2 tablespoons sugar

pinch salt

½ cup butter, melted

FILLING:

zest of 2 limes

4 egg yolks

2 (14-ounce) cans sweetened condensed milk

¾ cup lime juice

1 tablespoon tequila (optional)

DO AHEAD

FOR CRUST: Preheat oven to 350°F. Mix together the cookie crumbs, sugar, salt, and melted butter. Press into an 8- or 9-inch tart pan with a removeable bottom. Place on a baking sheet (in case some butter leaks out). Bake 8 to 10 minutes. Cool to room temperature.

FOR FILLING: Whisk the lime zest and egg yolks together. Whisk in the sweetened condensed milk, lime juice, and tequila (if using). Set aside a few minutes until slightly thickened. Pour into the prepared crust and bake 20 minutes. Cool to room temperature, then chill well, about 3 hours in the refrigerator.

Prep Time: 15 minutes

Cooking Time: 30 minutes

POMEGRANARITA

I'm a big-time margarita fan. Adding the magical antioxidant powerhouse pomegranate sort of balances out the effects of the alcohol, right? OK, maybe not, but it does add gorgeous color and flavor, and you can always make these sans *alcohol.*

FOR EACH DRINK:

3 tablespoons tequila

juice of 1 lime

2 tablespoons orange liqueur (Cointreau, Grand Marnier or other)

1 tablespoon simple syrup

3 tablespoons pomegranate juice or Pomegranate Limeade

lime wedge and pomegranate arils, for garnish

Fill a cocktail shaker with ice. Add all ingredients and shake. Rub rim of glass with lime wedge and dip rim in salt, if desired. Strain the shaker into a margarita glass. Garnish with lime wedge and pomegranate arils.

GRAB & GO
Cinco de Mayo No-Prep Snacks

There are tons of Latin-inspired products at TJ's. Salsas, sauces, handmade tortillas, and more await.

- CARNITAS
- HANDMADE TORTILLAS
- SALSAS AND GUACAMOLES

From the frozen section:

- BEEF, BEAN, AND CHEESE DIP
- TAQUITOS AND TAMALES
- GREEN CHILE AND CHEESE PUFFS

TAKE A HIKE

- ○ **ROAST BEEF WASABI ROLLS**
- ○ **CUCUMBER, RED ONION, AND KIDNEY BEAN SALAD**
- ○ **SATAY NOODLES**
- ○ **TRIPLE ALMOND BLONDIES**
- ○ **MUDDLED BASIL LIMEADE**

Picnic time? Whether your travels take you to the mountains, the lake, or just around the corner, a portable lunch makes the journey merry. If it's a spur of the moment jaunt, pick up crisp cold salads and premade sandwiches from a TJ's on the way. Don't forget the cookies!

ROAST BEEF WASABI ROLLS

These little three-bite wonders travel well in a backpack or picnic basket. The zippy wasabi perks up the flavors of the crunchy cucumbers and creamy avocado. After two or three of these babies, you'll be ready to do another three miles!

2 sheets whole wheat lavosh

2 to 4 tablespoons Trader Joe's Wasabi Mayonnaise

1 ripe avocado, thinly sliced

¼ red onion, thinly sliced

1 Persian cucumber, thinly sliced

about 10 slices roast beef

sprigs of mâche lettuce, for garnish (optional)

DO AHEAD

Spread one side of each lavosh sheet with wasabi mayonnaise. Scatter the avocado, red onion, and cucumber slices evenly over the lavosh. Arrange the slices of roast beef on the lavosh. Starting at one long end, roll each lavosh into a cylinder, encasing the fillings. Cut each roll in half, and then each half into four pieces. Garnish rolls with a sprig of mâche, if desired.

Prep Time: 10 minutes

Try to keep the rolls fairly tight and coax the fillings inside the lavosh as you go. Don't worry if you think you aren't rolling them perfectly—you can adjust them a little bit after they're sliced, and those sprigs of pretty, flowerlike mâche can cover up any imperfections beautifully!

CUCUMBER, RED ONION, and KIDNEY BEAN SALAD

I raised my kids on this salad—we ate it all summer long. It takes two shakes to toss together, it looks festive, and the flavors are cooling and refreshingly tart. The kids can throw it together while the burgers are grilling. It's a tip most moms know—if the kids help prepare the vegetables, they'll be more inclined to actually eat them, too!

½ an English or 3 Persian cucumbers, sliced

½ red onion, sliced into half-moons

1 (15-ounce) can kidney beans, drained and rinsed

3 tablespoons red wine vinegar

⅓ cup olive oil

salt and pepper

DO AHEAD
VEGAN, GLUTEN-FREE

In a large bowl, toss together all ingredients. Let flavors marry for at least 30 minutes, or as long as overnight, in the refrigerator.

Prep Time: 5 minutes

Put this salad in a resealable plastic bag, then put that bag inside another one. Pop some ice cubes into the outer bag, zip it tight, and the salad will stay crisp and chilled while you blaze the trail.

SATAY NOODLES

This colorful, crunchy tangle of noodle goodness is great hot, at room temperature, or chilled, so it's as good the second day as it is the day it's made—maybe better!

½ (13.2-ounce) package rice noodles

2 tablespoons grapeseed oil, divided

3 boneless, skinless chicken breasts, cut in strips

¼ red onion, thinly sliced

3 ribs celery, thinly sliced

handful of shredded carrots

1 (9-ounce) jar Trader Joe's Satay Peanut Sauce

sliced green onions, for garnish

DO AHEAD

In a pot of boiling water, cook the rice noodles until barely tender, about 8 minutes.

In a large sauté pan, heat 1 tablespoon of the oil and sauté the chicken strips, in batches, removing as the strips lose their pink color. When all the chicken has been sautéed, add it back to the pan, along with the remaining oil. When the oil is hot, add the onion and celery and sauté until softened. Add the shredded carrots and sauté an additional minute. Add the cooked noodles and the satay sauce and toss to combine. Garnish with green onions.

Prep Time: 10 minutes
Cooking Time: 15 minutes

TRIPLE ALMOND BLONDIES

There's just a touch of chocolate in these, so they won't melt all over the picnic basket. But they're just as satisfying as brownies, with a nutty aroma and a good chewy texture.

¾ cup crunchy almond butter

6 ounces (1½ sticks) butter, at room temperature

1 cup brown sugar

½ cup granulated sugar

2 eggs

1 teaspoon vanilla

1 cup Trader Joe's Multigrain Baking and Pancake Mix

¾ cup Trader Joe's Just Almond Meal

1 teaspoon baking powder

⅓ cup almond milk (or cow's milk)

½ cup chocolate chips

½ cup chopped dried cherries (optional)

DO AHEAD
VEGETARIAN

Preheat oven to 325°F. With an electric mixer, combine the almond butter, butter, brown sugar, and granulated sugar. Mix until fluffy and well combined. Add the eggs and vanilla. In a separate bowl, combine the baking mix, almond meal, and baking powder. Add about half the dry ingredients to the butter mixture, stirring by hand to incorporate. Add half the milk and stir in. Add the remaining dry ingredients, then stir in the remaining milk. Stir in chocolate chips and chopped cherries, if using. Grease a 9 x 13-inch baking pan and spoon batter into the pan, smoothing the top. Bake until set and golden, 40 to 45 minutes. Cool before cutting into squares.

Prep Time: 10 minutes
Cooking Time: 45 minutes

MUDDLED BASIL LIMEADE

This one's alcohol-free, but you aren't obligated to keep it that way! If you want to spike it, I'd recommend Burnett's Citrus Flavored Vodka or white rum.

FOR EACH DRINK:

4 fresh basil leaves

zest and juice of 2 limes

1 cup sparkling water

1 to 2 tablespoons simple syrup

ice

Place basil leaves in a tall glass and muddle them with a muddler or wooden spoon. Add the zest and juice of the limes. Add a few ice cubes and top with sparkling water. Sweeten to taste with simple syrup. Remove basil leaves and serve.

Freeze some premade TJ's limeade in ice cube trays. They'll keep a big batch of this refreshing beverage cold for a good, long hike, without watering down the drink.

MARTINI MADNESS

- VERMOUTH-GLAZED BEEF CROSTINI
- GRILLED GREEN OLIVE TAPENADE AND GOAT CHEESE PIZZETTAS
- MARTINI CHICKEN SKEWERS
- LEMON PUDDING CAKES WITH A TWIST
- CLASSIC MARTINI

Martinis come in and out of fashion every decade or two. I think the show *Mad Men* may be responsible for the latest resurgence. I can't handle a three-martini lunch, but a party with some of these tasty morsels? We're on!

VERMOUTH-GLAZED BEEF CROSTINI

So simple, so satisfying. The mustard and capers add a zingy element to the deep beefy flavor. Make mine extra-rare, please.

3 tablespoons butter, divided

1 pound filet mignon, at room temperature

3 tablespoons vermouth

1 tablespoon whole grain Dijon mustard

1 tablespoon capers, drained

salt and pepper

½ a baguette, sliced into rounds

In a medium sauté pan over high heat, melt 1 tablespoon of butter. Season the beef with salt and pepper, and cook until rare, 3 to 5 minutes per side, depending upon thickness. Remove from pan and let rest at least 10 minutes before slicing. While meat rests, add the remaining 2 tablespoons butter and the vermouth to the pan, and bring to a simmer. Simmer until thickened, about 4 minutes. Slice the beef thin and return any juices to the pan, along with the mustard and capers. If the beef is too rare, return the slices to the pan with the sauce and simmer until desired degree of doneness is achieved. Season meat and sauce with salt and pepper. Drizzle a little sauce over each bread slice, and top with a slice of beef. Top with a little more sauce.

Prep Time: 10 minutes
Cooking Time: 15 minutes

GRILLED GREEN OLIVE TAPENADE *and* GOAT CHEESE PIZZETTAS

Grilled pizza is so easy, and makes you look like a rock star to friends who don't know how simple it is! Another party idea is to make a grilled-pizza bar, with tons of pestos, spreads, sun-dried tomatoes, cheeses, and other toppings. Let everyone go nuts creating inspired flavor combinations, and award a be-ribboned pizza cutter to the creator of the most delicious one!

1 pound whole-wheat pizza dough

1 (10-ounce) jar Trader Joe's Green Olive Tapenade (or another pesto or spread)

3 ounces goat cheese

VEGETARIAN

Bring the pizza dough out of the refrigerator about 15 minutes before you shape it (the dough will be much easier to form into rounds if it's not completely chilled). Preheat grill to medium heat. Divide pizza dough into four pieces and form into flattened rounds, about 6 inches in diameter. Place the pizzettas on the grill and cook about 4 minutes, until grill marks form and dough looks cooked on the bottom. Flip the pizzettas and cook on the other side about 4 more minutes. If the dough starts to puff too much, pierce it with a skewer or knife point to deflate. When the dough is nearly cooked through, spread a tablespoon or so of tapenade on each pizzetta and top with a few teaspoons of goat cheese. Close the grill lid and cook about 2 minutes, until toppings are warm. Cut in quarters and serve.

Prep Time: 10 minutes
Cooking Time: 10 minutes

....

You can use regular or garlic-and-herb pizza dough for this, of course. And if it's not grilling weather, you can bake them in the oven. A pizza stone will help make a crispy, toothsome crust.

....

MARTINI CHICKEN SKEWERS

Classic martini flavors on a skewer. TJ's doesn't sell jarred cocktail onions, but if you happen to have some on hand, thread a few onto each stick.

1 pound boneless, skinless chicken breasts or thighs, cut into bite-sized cubes

¼ cup olive oil

2 tablespoons gin

1 tablespoon vermouth

1 tablespoon chopped rosemary

zest of 1 lemon

1 jar green olives

1 red onion, quartered and sliced

GLUTEN-FREE

Combine chicken, olive oil, gin, vermouth, rosemary, and lemon zest in a resealable plastic bag. Marinate at least 2 hours, or overnight in the refrigerator. Heat a medium sauté pan over high heat, place all the chicken and marinade in the pan, and sauté until chicken is cooked through and coated with glaze, about 7 minutes.

Skewer the chicken, alternating with olives and onion pieces.

Prep Time: 10 minutes
Cooking Time: 10 minutes

LEMON PUDDING CAKES
with a TWIST

Light, bright, and lemony, this is the perfect dessert for a martini evening. The cakes will rise like soufflés, but then they'll sink, so don't be dismayed. The flavor is terrifically tart.

1 tablespoon butter, melted

2 tablespoons flour

pinch salt

¼ cup plus 2 tablespoons sugar

2 eggs, separated

½ cup milk

juice and zest of 1 lemon, plus zest of another lemon, for garnish

powdered sugar, for garnish

VEGETARIAN

Preheat oven to 375°F. Butter four ramekins or a 1-quart baking dish with the melted butter. In a large bowl, combine flour, salt, and ¼ cup sugar. In another bowl, whisk together egg yolks, milk, and lemon zest and juice. Whisk into flour mixture, just until incorporated. With an electric mixer, whisk the egg whites to soft peaks. Sprinkle in the remaining 2 tablespoons sugar, a little at a time, until sugar is incorporated and whites are glossy. Fold ⅓ of the whites into the lemon mixture, incorporating well. Fold half of the remaining whites into the lemon mixture, and then fold in the rest. Fill prepared ramekins or baking dish, place on a baking sheet, and bake until puffy and browned, about 20 minutes for ramekins, and 40 for baking dish. Dust with powdered sugar and additional lemon zest.

Prep Time: 20 minutes

Cooking Time: 20 minutes (if using ramekins) or 40 minutes (for a large baking dish)

For a martini-appropriate garnish, cut strips of lemon zest from the "garnish" lemon. A channel knife works best for this—it's a bartender's tool. (Alternately, use a vegetable peeler to remove swaths of zest, then cut narrow strips with a knife.) Tie strips into knots and use them to garnish each ramekin. It that's crazy-making, just sprinkle some zest on top!

CLASSIC MARTINI

There are so many martini variations out there, but I'm just givin' you the hard-core, old-school version. Legend has it that it was created in Martinez, California, mixed for a thirsty miner. I like that story, so I'm sticking to it—and to this potent sipper. In the classic film The Thin Man, *William Powell's suave Nick Charles discloses that the shaking of a martini should be done to waltz tempo.*

FOR EACH DRINK:
¼ cup gin
1 teaspoon dry vermouth
ice cubes
lemon twist or green olive

Fill a cocktail shaker with ice cubes. Pour in the gin and vermouth and shake. Strain into martini glass and garnish with a lemon twist or olive.

MOTHER'S DAY BRUNCH

- ○ **FRENCHER-THAN-FRENCH TOAST**
- ○ **TACO 'TATERS**
- ○ **CANDIED BACON**
- ○ **MOJITO FRUIT SALAD**
- ○ **RICOTTA BABY CAKES WITH BERRIES**
- ○ **MOM-OSA**

While its title is Mother's Day Brunch, don't limit this menu to one day in May. This bouquet of recipes contains what I consider to be the critical brunch elements: something carb-y, something egg-y, something fruity, a pretty drink, and some bacon! It makes a great brunch spread any time of the year, so make it for Mom, but don't stop there.

FRENCHER-THAN-FRENCH TOAST

The technique for this recipe was inspired by a fabulous blog, Chocolate and Zucchini. *Its author, Clotilde Dusoulier, makes everything she writes about sound delicious. This recipe, whether made with almonds, as Clotilde does it, or hazelnuts and raspberries, is no different. Happily, it tastes even better than it sounds, if that's even possible.*

4 day-old croissants

⅔ cup toasted hazelnuts, skins rubbed off

½ cup sugar

4 ounces butter

2 eggs

2 tablespoons simple syrup

1 tablespoon Frangelico

¼ cup Trader Joe's Fresh Raspberry Preserves

a few chopped hazelnuts and powdered sugar, for garnish

DO AHEAD
(assemble, refrigerate until ready to bake; increase baking time by 10 to 15 minutes, depending on how cold the dish is)
VEGETARIAN

Preheat oven to 375°F. Cut the croissants in half, from end to end. Toast lightly. In a food processor, pulse the hazelnuts with sugar until finely ground. Add the butter and pulse again to combine. Add the eggs and process until smooth. Set aside.

Stir the simple syrup and Frangelico together. Dip the baked sides (not the cut sides) of each croissant half into the Frangelico syrup. Place the croissant bottoms, syrup-side down, in an ovenproof casserole dish large enough to hold the croissants in a single layer. Spread about 2 tablespoons of the hazelnut-butter mixture on each bottom. Spread the cut side of the croissant tops with the raspberry jam. Put croissant tops on, and spread each with a little more of the hazelnut-butter mixture. Sprinkle with the chopped hazelnuts and bake until filling is set and golden, about 15 minutes. Sprinkle with powdered sugar and serve.

Prep Time: 30 minutes
Cooking Time: 15 minutes

TACO 'TATERS

A quintet of good-for-you veggies in one tasty, colorful treat.
Wait 'til you see how vibrant this looks on a platter—you'll
be making this over and over again!

1 pound red-skinned
potatoes, cubed

1 pound yellow-skinned
potatoes, cubed

1 (12-ounce) package Trader
Joe's Sweet Potato Spears

1 pint Trader Joe's Minisweet
Bell Peppers, chopped

1 red onion, thickly sliced

4 tablespoons olive oil

2 tablespoons Trader Joe's Taco
Seasoning Mix

1 cup Trader Joe's Pepper Jack
Shredded Cheese Blend

salt and pepper

DO AHEAD (assemble up to
point of roasting)
VEGETARIAN, GLUTEN-FREE

Preheat oven to 400°F. In a large bowl, combine the
cubed potatoes, sweet potato spears, chopped bell
pepper, and red onion. Toss with the olive oil. Sprinkle
with taco seasoning, salt, and pepper, and toss well
to distribute seasoning. Arrange the vegetables on a
rimmed baking sheet in a single layer. Roast 30 to 35
minutes, until potatoes are tender. Scatter shredded
cheese over the vegetables, and return briefly to the oven
to melt the cheese.

Prep Time: 10 minutes
Cooking Time: 35 minutes

....

If you're a chile-head, add some canned Hatch Valley Fire-Roasted
Diced Green Chiles to the pan when you add the cheese. Yowza!

....

CANDIED BACON

Bacon's gotten so popular in the past few years that I've seen it on several "What's In, What's Out" lists in the "Out" column. It's not on my "out" list...ever!

12 slices (1 12-ounce package) Niman Ranch Applewood Smoked Dry-Cured Bacon

¼ cup brown sugar

pinch of cayenne pepper

GLUTEN-FREE

Preheat oven to 450°F. Stir together the brown sugar and cayenne pepper. Spread bacon slices on a cooling rack on a cookie sheet and sprinkle evenly with brown sugar mixture. Bake until bacon is cooked and glazed, about 20 minutes.

Prep Time: 5 minutes
Cooking Time: 20 minutes

Cookware stores sell cooling racks that fit inside baking sheets. They're wire grids, and they work really well for baking bacon nice and flat, and letting some grease drain off.

MOJITO FRUIT SALAD

The first time we served this at the cooking school, there was an audible gasp of appreciation from the crowd. Within a week, two of my teachers had prepared it for family and friends—all sure signs of a winning recipe!

4 cups diced fruit (pears, plums, apricots, melons, berries— whatever looks great in the market)

2 to 3 tablespoons simple syrup

1 to 2 tablespoons rum

juice of 2 limes

¼ cup chopped fresh mint

DO AHEAD
VEGAN, GLUTEN-FREE

Toss all ingredients together in a glass bowl. Let stand at room temperature at least 20 minutes to let flavors meld.

Prep Time: 10 minutes

RICOTTA BABY CAKES
with BERRIES

I saw a variation of this recipe online, and based on the rave reviews, I had to give it a whirl, even though I'm generally not a cake person. (Nine times out of ten, I'll take cheese over cake!) The original recipe was attributed to Gina DePalma, pastry chef at Babbo in Manhattan. If her version is anything like this, I'll go for the cake if I ever make it to Babbo.

about 2 tablespoons butter, melted

6 ounces butter, at room temperature

1½ cups sugar

1 (15-ounce) container whole-milk ricotta cheese

3 eggs

1 teaspoon vanilla

zest and juice of 1 lemon

1½ cups flour

1 tablespoon baking powder

pinch salt

blueberries, raspberries, and sliced strawberries, for garnish

powdered sugar, for garnish

DO AHEAD
VEGETARIAN

Preheat oven to 350°F. Brush a muffin tin well with the melted butter. With an electric mixer, cream together the butter, sugar, and ricotta. Add the eggs, one at a time, incorporating well. Add the vanilla and lemon zest and juice and combine. Sift together the flour, baking powder, and salt. Stir the dry ingredients into the ricotta mixture, just to combine well. Spoon batter into the buttered muffin tin and bake until golden, 20 minutes. Cool the baby cakes in the pan 10 minutes before unmolding. For garnish, combine the berries with a little powdered sugar and serve with the baby cakes.

Prep Time: 15 minutes
Cooking Time: 20 minutes

MOM-OSA

I love the tang and blush of the grapefruit juice. It tastes perfect with brunch fare.

FOR EACH DRINK:

1 ounce fresh-squeezed pink grapefruit juice

2 teaspoons Trader Joe's Organic Blue Agave Syrup

champagne or sparkling wine

In a champagne flute, pour the grapefruit juice. Add agave syrup and top with champagne or sparkling wine. Stir gently.

GRAB & GO
No-Prep Mother's Day Brunch

Of course, you can always grab eggs for scrambling and bacon, well, for baconing, but there are lots more inventive ideas waiting for you at Joe's.

- TRADER JOE'S SWEET APPLE CHICKEN SAUSAGES (PRECOOKED, BUT SAUTÉ WITH A LITTLE MAPLE SYRUP AND MUSTARD)

From the frozen section:

- MINI CROISSANTS AND CHOCOLATE CROISSANTS (I CAN'T BEGIN TO EXPRESS HOW GREAT THESE ARE! GO NOW!)
- POTATO LATKES
- HASHBROWNS
- POPOVERS

SUEÑOS DE ESPAÑA

- ROASTED MUSHROOM EMPANADILLAS
- BLOOD ORANGE AND ALMOND SALAD
- ALCACHOFAS EN BUFANDA
- SHRIMP, SPUDS, AND GREEN BEANS WITH RED PEPPER SAUCE
- VALENCIA ALMOND CAKE WITH HONEYED MASCARPONE
- SANGRIA

If your budget won't allow a sunny Spanish holiday, put some flamenco on the iPod and imagine yourself on the Costa del Sol. Invite a few friends to join you on the terrace—real or imagined—to sip sangria or Rioja, and you're halfway there.

ROASTED MUSHROOM EMPANADILLAS

There are a million different fillings you can substitute for the mushrooms in these mini empanadas. Chopped, cooked chicken and olives, roast pork and a little spicy tomato sauce, my beloved Trader Joe's Corn and Chile Tomato-Less Salsa and feta...these are fun for guests to assemble over a glass of wine, so put your friends to work!

½ pound assorted fresh mushrooms

2 cubes frozen garlic

1 tablespoon olive oil

2 tablespoons crème fraîche

2 Trader Joe's Gourmet Pie Crusts, thawed

1 egg, beaten with a tablespoon of water (optional)

salt, pepper, and crushed red chile pepper flakes, to taste

DO AHEAD
VEGETARIAN

Preheat oven to 400°F. Toss the mushrooms and garlic with olive oil, salt, pepper, and a pinch of crushed red chile pepper flakes. Place on a rimmed baking sheet and roast until tender and fragrant, about 15 minutes. Cool the mushrooms to room temperature, then coarsely chop. Stir in the crème fraîche. Adjust seasoning to taste.

Roll out pie crust and cut into 3-inch rounds. (You can re-roll the crust once, and should be able to get a dozen rounds from each crust.) Place about a teaspoon of chopped mushroom filling in the center of each pastry round, fold in half, and crimp edges tightly to seal. Place on a parchment-lined baking sheet and brush with egg wash, if desired (the egg wash will give the pastry a shiny appearance). Bake until pastry is golden, about 18 minutes.

Prep Time: 10 minutes
Cooking Time: 40 minutes

If you don't seal the edges firmly, the empanadillas may pop open while baking. Never fear—those ones look like tiny tacos, and they taste just as terrific.

BLOOD ORANGE *and* ALMOND SALAD

Use the leftover orange juice from this salad for your sangria or in a glass of Cava—the Champagne of Spain.

½ (7-ounce) bag arugula

2 blood oranges (or navel oranges, or clementines, if blood oranges aren't in season)

½ red onion, thinly sliced

3 tablespoons olive oil

salt and pepper

handful of Marcona almonds

VEGAN, GLUTEN-FREE

Arrange the arugula on individual plates or a platter. Peel and cut one of the oranges in half, and then into half moons to get about 10 to 12 slices, and arrange them on the plates or platter. Scatter the red onion over the salad. Zest the remaining orange and then juice it. Place the zest and 1 tablespoon of the juice in a bowl and whisk in the olive oil. Taste the dressing on a leaf of arugula, and season to taste with salt and pepper. (Arugula is peppery, so you won't need much pepper.) Drizzle the dressing over the salad and divide the almonds among the salads.

Prep Time: 10 minutes

ALCACHOFAS EN BUFANDA

Artichokes in scarves! Well, of course...it's a party, after all. They'd want to look their best, and the delicious scarves are made of deftly draped swaths of prosciutto.

1 (14.6-ounce) jar Trader Joe's Artichokes with Stems

about 4 slices provolone

about 8 slices prosciutto

DO AHEAD
GLUTEN-FREE

Preheat oven to 400°F. Cut four artichokes in half lengthwise. Cut each slice of provolone in half. Place a slice of prosciutto on a cutting board and put a half-slice of provolone on top. Set an artichoke half on top of the cheese, and wind the cheese and prosciutto around the artichoke. Place on a parchment-lined baking sheet. Repeat with remaining artichoke halves. Bake until the cheese is melty and the prosciutto is a little browned, about 8 minutes. Cool slightly before serving.

Prep Time: 10 minutes
Cooking Time: 10 minutes

SHRIMP, SPUDS, and GREEN BEANS with RED PEPPER SAUCE

Here's a one-dish meal that looks fancy but is quick and easy to put together, and it's good for you, too! That's a winner in my book, every time.

1 pound Teeny Tiny Potatoes (or other thin-skinned potatoes, cubed)

1 to 2 tablespoons olive oil

1 pound medium-sized raw shrimp, thawed, peeled, and deveined

1 (8-ounce) bag fresh (not frozen) haricots verts (French green beans)

salt and pepper

SAUCE:

½ cup walnut pieces, toasted

2 cubes frozen garlic

1 (10.4-ounce) jar Roasted Piquillo Peppers, drained

1 tablespoon balsamic vinegar

1 tablespoon lemon juice

½ teaspoon cumin, toasted and ground

1 teaspoon honey

salt and pepper

DO AHEAD
GLUTEN-FREE

Preheat oven to 425°F. Toss the potatoes with some olive oil and place on a rimmed baking sheet. Roast until the potatoes are nearly tender, about 20 minutes. Add the shrimp and green beans to the pan, season with salt and pepper, and roast until the shrimp are pink and the green beans are tender, about 10 minutes. While the potatoes roast, make the red pepper sauce.

FOR SAUCE: While the potatoes roast, place the walnut pieces and garlic in the bowl of a food processor and process until finely chopped. Add the peppers, vinegar, lemon juice, cumin, and honey, and process until well combined. Season to taste with salt and pepper. When the potatoes, shrimp, and green beans are cooked, toss with the red pepper sauce.

Prep Time: 15 minutes
Cooking Time: 30 minutes

If the piquillo peppers aren't available (and you haven't hoarded them when they were!), substitute about a jar of roasted red bell peppers.

VALENCIA ALMOND CAKE
with HONEYED MASCARPONE

This rustic dessert goes well with a glass of sherry or port. The almonds and oranges are typical Spanish flavors, and the cake keeps well for several days. (It's great for breakfast, I happen to know.)

1 (8-ounce) package blanched almonds, or 2 cups Trader Joe's Just Almond Meal

½ cup sugar, divided

4 eggs, separated

zest of 2 oranges

pinch of salt

2 tablespoons Amontillado Sherry

powdered sugar, for garnish

DO AHEAD
VEGETARIAN, GLUTEN-FREE

Preheat oven to 375°F. Butter a 9-inch cake pan. If using blanched almonds, place the almonds in a food processor with 2 tablespoons of the sugar. Pulse until the almonds are finely ground. Set aside. (If using almond meal, combine the meal with 2 tablespoons of sugar and set aside.) With an electric mixer, beat the egg yolks with another 2 tablespoons of sugar. Add the orange zest and the salt, and beat 2 minutes. Stir the sherry into the ground almonds, then combine this mixture with the yolk mixture. With an electric mixer, beat the egg whites until soft peaks form. Sprinkle in the remaining 4 tablespoons sugar, a tablespoon at a time, until incorporated.

Add half the egg whites to the almond–egg yolk mixture and stir to combine. Add the rest of the whites and fold gently to combine. Spoon into the prepared cake pan and bake 30 to 35 minutes, until a skewer inserted into the center comes out clean. Cool 10 minutes before removing from pan. Cool completely, and dust with powdered sugar. Serve with Honeyed Mascarpone (page 136).

Prep Time: 15 minutes
Cooking Time: 40 minutes

The ground almonds take the place of flour in this cake, so it's a great trick to have up your sleeve for gluten-free folks. Grind the almonds very finely, as the recipe indicates, for a pound-cake-like texture. Or leave them a little on the coarse side, for a nuttier, crumblier result. I like both!

HONEYED MASCARPONE

My bestie, Chris, one of my right-hand kitchen goddesses, "pre-requested" a bowl of this goodness and a spoon for her post-baby-delivery hospital stay after baby number two! It's that good.

1 (8-ounce) container
mascarpone, at room
temperature

1 to 2 tablespoons honey

1 tablespoon Marsala (optional)

DO AHEAD
VEGETARIAN, GLUTEN-FREE

Stir together the mascarpone and enough honey to sweeten it to taste. Stir in the Marsala, if using.

Prep Time: 5 minutes

SANGRIA

This is a sangria for all seasons—there are always citrus fruits around. But in summer, kick it up a notch with lusciously ripe peach or plum chunks, berries, or whatever fruit sounds good to you. Grapes? Melon balls? I say go for it.

1 bottle Rioja (or another
light-bodied red wine)

1½ cups mineral water

2 ounces brandy

2 tablespoons sugar
or simple syrup

1 lime, sliced

1 lemon, sliced

1 orange, sliced

Combine all ingredients in a large glass pitcher and stir to dissolve sugar (if not using simple syrup). Chill or serve over ice.

FATHER'S DAY AT THE GRILL

- GREEN BEANS AND POTATOES WITH CHERRY TOMATOES AND PESTO
- TROPICAL TSAO SKEWERS
- COFFEE-RUBBED RIB-EYES
- BBQ BLACK BEANS WITH BACON
- RASPBERRY RIPPLE ICE CREAM PIE
- SODA SHOP FLOATS

Whether Dad wants to man the grill himself or sit back and direct the action, this menu will have him feeling like a proud papa, for sure. Meat and potatoes, not too gussied up, but with a little twist thrown in here and there to keep things interesting—this is summer food, man-style.

GREEN BEANS *and* POTATOES *with* CHERRY TOMATOES *and* PESTO

This dish looks like summer to me—the double green of the beans and pesto, the popping red dots of tomato, punctuated by the creamy white feta...primary colors and primal taste on one platter!

½ (1-pound) bag Teeny Tiny Potatoes (or ½ pound other smooth-skinned, waxy potatoes, like Red Bliss, cut into 2-inch cubes)

1 pound green beans, trimmed

1 (7-ounce) container Trader Giotto's Genova Pesto (in the refrigerated section)

1 cup Trader Joe's Mixed Medley Cherry Tomatoes or Mini Heirloom Tomatoes, halved

½ (8-ounce) package feta cheese, crumbled

DO AHEAD
VEGETARIAN, GLUTEN-FREE

Bring a large pot of salted water to a boil. Add the potatoes and cook 5 minutes. Add the green beans and cook until the beans and potatoes are tender, about 7 minutes. Drain. Toss the potatoes and green beans with the pesto, coating well. Arrange vegetables on a platter and garnish with cherry tomatoes and crumbled feta.

Prep Time: 10 minutes
Cooking Time: 15 minutes

TROPICAL TSAO SKEWERS

Simple, pretty, and quick! What more can you ask for in an appetizer?

1 (12-ounce) package precooked Trader Joe's Mango Chicken sausage

½ cup Trader Ming's General Tsao Stir-Fry Sauce or Bold and Smoky Kansas City Style Barbecue Sauce

1 (16-ounce) container fresh pineapple spears, or half pineapple and half mango

DO AHEAD (assemble and refrigerate until you're ready to grill)

Soak bamboo skewers in water for 30 minutes. Preheat grill to medium heat. Cut the sausages into bite-sized pieces (about six pieces per sausage). Skewer, alternating pineapple chunks and sausage. Brush with General Tsao sauce (or barbecue sauce). Grill 2 to 3 minutes per side, until warmed through and with great grill marks. Serve skewers by themselves, or atop salad greens.

Prep Time: 10 minutes
Cooking Time: 10 minutes

These are great with shrimp instead of, or in addition to, the sausage.

Here's a little trick that will make your skewering life a joy: Instead of using a single bamboo skewer, use two, side by side. When you double-skewer your ingredients, they'll lay flat on your grates and will turn easily, rather than flop around on the stick when you try to flip them over.

COFFEE-RUBBED RIB-EYES

The smoky depth of this rub pairs really well with the rich beefiness, and as it chars, it creates a toothsome, crunchy crust. Yum!

1 tablespoon Trader Joe's Taco Seasoning Mix

1 tablespoon espresso coffee grounds

2 teaspoons ground cumin

1 teaspoon dried oregano

1 tablespoon salt

1½ teaspoons freshly ground black pepper

4 (8-ounce) rib-eye steaks, at room temperature

GLUTEN-FREE

Preheat a grill or broiler to medium-high heat. Mix all dry ingredients together. Press the mixture onto both sides of steaks. Grill or broil steaks to desired degree of doneness—3 to 4 minutes per side for rare, 4 to 5 for medium, 6 for well-done.

Prep Time: 5 minutes
Cooking Time: 15 minutes

Good Griller's Rule: Let steaks rest 5 to 10 minutes before slicing so juices redistribute throughout the meat. Otherwise, all the juicy goodness runs out and you gotta chase it with your garlic bread!

BBQ BLACK BEANS *with* BACON

You can punch these babies up with hot sauce or red chile pepper flakes, if you like things really spicy. They're great wrapped in a tortilla, too.

4 strips Niman Ranch Applewood Smoked Dry-Cured Bacon, chopped

1 cup chopped onion

6 Trader Joe's Minisweet Bell Peppers, chopped

3 cubes frozen garlic

2 cans black beans, drained and rinsed

½ to 1 cup Bold and Smoky Kansas City Style Barbecue Sauce (depending on how "soupy" you like your beans)

salt and pepper

DO AHEAD

In a medium sauté pan, cook the bacon until nearly crisp. Remove from pan with a slotted spoon and reserve. In the bacon fat, sauté the chopped onion until translucent, about 4 minutes. Add the peppers and sauté 3 to 4 minutes, until tender. Add the garlic and sauté 1 to 2 minutes, until fragrant. Add the drained black beans and barbecue sauce and warm through. Season to taste with salt and pepper.

Prep Time: 10 minutes
Cooking Time: 20 minutes

Does chopping onions make you cry? TJ's has prechopped onions in a bag. If you're a tough guy like me and chop your own, don't measure the onion in this recipe—just chop one up!

RASPBERRY RIPPLE ICE CREAM PIE

This is one of those "template" recipes—use a different cookie, use a different ice cream, add some chocolate (never a bad idea) or whatever strikes your fancy. Easy + pretty + tasty = fun!

2 cups cookie crumbs
(I like Triple Ginger Snaps)

2 tablespoon butter, melted

1 quart vanilla ice cream,
softened

½ cup Trader Joe's Fresh
Raspberry Preserves

1 pint fresh raspberries

**DO AHEAD
VEGETARIAN**

Preheat oven to 350°F. In a plastic bag or bowl, mix together the crumbs and melted butter until they look like wet sand. Press the crumbs evenly over the bottom and up the sides of a 9-inch pie pan. Bake 10 minutes. Cool completely before filling. With an electric mixer, combine the ice cream and jam—you can mix thoroughly or just swirl the jam through. Fill the cooled crust with the ice cream mixture and freeze, at least 2 hours. Scatter the fresh berries over the top of the pie before serving.

Prep Time: 10 minutes
Cooking Time: 10 minutes

For a crowd, do these in cupcake form instead. Use cute cupcake papers in a muffin tin. Press about ¼ cup of crumb mixture into the bottom of each one and bake as directed. Divide the ice cream mixture evenly among the cupcake papers and freeze. The recipe will make about 18 ice cream cupcakes.

SODA SHOP FLOATS

Pour Dad a frosty glass of whatever he likes to drink on his day! These are for the kid in all of us.

vanilla ice cream

Virgil's Rootbeer, Reed's Extra Ginger Brew Ginger Beer, or orange soda

For each drink, place a scoop of vanilla ice cream in a tall glass and top it with your soda of choice.

SUNSET AT THE SHORE

- CRAB CONES
- ROASTED SHRIMP SALAD
- BERRY SHORE-T CAKES
- SEA BREEZE

I grew up near the sound of the Pacific, and I feel soothed whenever I can see or hear the waves breaking. We rent a beach house every year, and having sandy-footed friends and family around is my idea of bliss. We keep the grill fired up and eat lots of fresh seafood. This menu is very portable, so you can pack it into the car and head toward the setting sun. No shoes allowed while you enjoy these treats!

CRAB CONES

These little cones of crabby goodness are portable and posh. Wrap a piece of parchment paper or a paper napkin around them to contain the drips.

1 sheet lavosh

¼ cup organic mayonnaise

1 tablespoon Trader Joe's Sweet Chili Sauce

1 ripe avocado, sliced

1 ripe mango, sliced

1 Persian cucumber, sliced

½ (16-ounce) can refrigerated crab meat

salt, pepper, and lime juice

Cut the lavosh sheet into 4 squares. Stir together the mayonnaise and sweet chili sauce and spread lightly over the surface of the lavosh squares. Place a few slices of avocado, mango, and cucumber on each square, and top with crab. Season with salt and pepper and a squeeze of lime juice. Starting at one corner, carefully roll the lavosh into a cone, making sure the bottom is tightly closed (to avoid dripping). Secure with a toothpick. Repeat with remaining lavosh.

Prep Time: 15 minutes

I love the presentation of these cute crab cones, but you can make it easy on yourself by using pita pockets, if you like. Wasabi Mayonnaise is great in place of the sweet chili mayo, too.

ROASTED SHRIMP SALAD

Thank you, Ina Garten, for the tip about roasting shrimp instead of boiling it. She does this for her shrimp cocktails, and she's right—the depth of flavor is much greater. Makes sense—roasting intensifies flavors, while boiling dilutes them. And any time you cook shrimp in their shells, you get even more flavor.

1 pound frozen shell-on raw shrimp, thawed

1 tablespoon olive oil

½ cup organic mayonnaise

2 teaspoons Trader Joe's Aioli Garlic Mustard Sauce

¼ red onion, chopped

2 green onions, chopped

2 ribs celery, chopped

salt, pepper, and dried dill

½ (7-ounce) bag butter lettuce

Preheat oven to 400°F. Toss shrimp with olive oil and arrange in a single layer on a baking sheet. Roast until shrimp are pink throughout, 8 to 10 minutes. Cool and peel. Roughly chop the shrimp and combine in a bowl with the mayonnaise, aioli, onions, and celery. Season to taste with salt, pepper, and dill. Serve on a bed of butter lettuce leaves.

Prep Time: 10 minutes
Cooking Time: 10 minutes

BERRY SHORE-T CAKES

Packable and portable, these tasty treats are not short on flavor. Use the freshest, most flavorful berries you can get your hands on. The whole container of biscuits will make eight shortcakes, so if you're cooking for four people, you'll have leftovers for breakfast!

1 (16-ounce) container Trader Joe's Buttermilk Biscuits (in the refrigerated case)

¼ cup butter, melted

½ cup turbinado sugar

2 cups fresh berries (raspberries, blackberries, blueberries, and sliced strawberries are all good choices, or use a combination)

1 to 2 tablespoons sugar or Trader Joe's Organic Blue Agave Syrup

a can of whipped cream (see note)

DO AHEAD
VEGETARIAN

Preheat oven to 350°F. Dip both flat sides of each biscuit into the butter and then into the turbinado sugar. Place on parchment-lined baking sheet. Bake until sugar is golden and biscuits are baked through, about 20 minutes. While biscuits bake, sweeten the berries to taste. When ready to serve, split the biscuits in half, spoon some berries on each bottom, squirt with some whipped cream and top with the biscuit top.

Prep Time: 10 minutes
Cooking Time: 20 minutes

If you're packing these to take to a beach supper, tuck the unsplit biscuits in one container and the berries in another. You can just pull the biscuits apart with your fingers, or split them with a picnic knife, and assemble them on the spot.

Hey, I never use whipped topping, but this is the real deal, and it makes these so much more portable. Use real cream you've whipped yourself if you're in the comfort of your own kitchen, by all means!

SEA BREEZE

Love the color of this simple and simply delicious drink—the fresh grapefruit juice adds a terrific bright flavor.

FOR EACH DRINK:
1½ ounces vodka
¼ cup fresh grapefruit juice
¼ cup cranberry juice
ice

In a cocktail glass with ice, pour in the vodka and top with grapefruit juice and cranberry juice. Stir.

FOURTH OF JULY

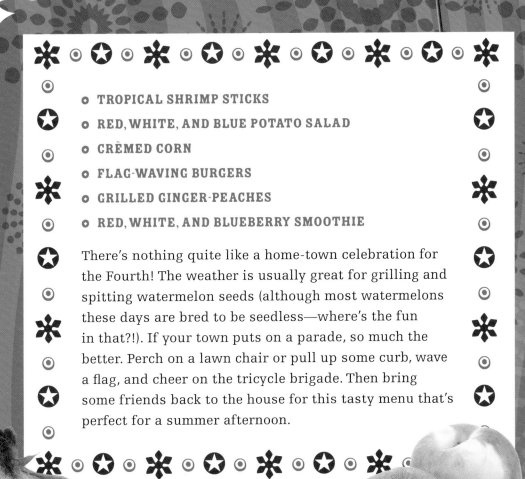

- **TROPICAL SHRIMP STICKS**
- **RED, WHITE, AND BLUE POTATO SALAD**
- **CRÈMED CORN**
- **FLAG-WAVING BURGERS**
- **GRILLED GINGER-PEACHES**
- **RED, WHITE, AND BLUEBERRY SMOOTHIE**

There's nothing quite like a home-town celebration for the Fourth! The weather is usually great for grilling and spitting watermelon seeds (although most watermelons these days are bred to be seedless—where's the fun in that?!). If your town puts on a parade, so much the better. Perch on a lawn chair or pull up some curb, wave a flag, and cheer on the tricycle brigade. Then bring some friends back to the house for this tasty menu that's perfect for a summer afternoon.

TROPICAL SHRIMP STICKS

These zingy bites will get the party started—they look so tropically summery, and their flavor is bright and citrusy. You might want to skip the burgers and just eat these with some Basil and Corn Rice (you'll find that recipe in the I Love Trader Joe's Cookbook*).*

1 pound frozen raw medium tail-on shrimp, thawed

juice of 2 limes, plus 2 additional limes, thinly sliced, for garnish

1 tablespoon honey or Trader Joe's Organic Blue Agave Sweetener

several shakes of Trader Joe's Chili Pepper Hot Sauce or Jalapeño Pepper Hot Sauce

2 cups mango and/or pineapple cubes

salt and pepper

DO AHEAD
GLUTEN-FREE

Preheat a grill to high heat and soak about 30 bamboo skewers in water for 20 minutes prior to skewering the food. In a large bowl, toss shrimp, lime juice, honey or agave syrup, hot sauce, and fruit cubes. Assemble the skewers, alternating shrimp and fruit. Garnish each skewer with a lime slice. Grill about 3 minutes per side, until shrimp is pink. Season with salt and pepper.

Prep Time: 10 minutes
Cooking Time: 10 minutes

Instead of using a single bamboo skewer, use two, side by side. This will help your ingredients lay flat on the grill and make flipping them over a breeze.

RED, WHITE, and BLUE POTATO SALAD

These tricolor, thin-skinned baby potatoes hold together when cooked, which is what I want for potato salad. You can switch the seasonings up by adding a little mint, some bacon, or barbecue sauce.

1 pound Trader Joe's Potato Medley, or a mixture of red, white, and blue (purple) boiling potatoes, whole, quartered, or cubed, depending upon size

¼ cup crème fraîche

¼ cup mayonnaise

2 tablespoons Trader Joe's Aioli Garlic Mustard Sauce

4 green onions, chopped

½ red onion, chopped

¼ cup chopped fresh basil

2 tablespoons capers

salt and pepper

DO AHEAD
VEGETARIAN

Bring a large pot of salted water to a boil. Add potatoes and cook until a skewer penetrates the potatoes easily but they retain a slight firmness. Drain. Combine crème fraîche, mayonnaise, and aioli sauce. Add to warm potatoes and toss to combine. Add chopped green and red onions, basil, and capers and toss again. Season to taste with salt and pepper. Serve at room temperature or chilled.

Prep Time: 10 minutes
Cooking Time: 15 minutes

CRÈMED CORN

This dish is full of creamy, corny goodness, with a smoky bacon flavor that will make you grateful for corn season.

3 strips bacon, chopped

1 shallot, chopped

1½ cups fresh corn kernels (from about 4 ears)

¼ cup crème fraîche

1 to 2 teaspoons Trader Joe's Chili Pepper Hot Sauce or Jalapeño Pepper Hot Sauce

DO AHEAD
GLUTEN-FREE

In a medium sauté pan, cook the chopped bacon until it's opaque but not completely crisp. Add the shallot and sauté until fragrant. Add the corn kernels and sauté 2 to 3 minutes. Add the crème fraîche and hot sauce. Adjust seasoning with more hot sauce, salt, and pepper to taste.

Prep Time: 10 minutes
Cooking Time: 10 minutes

FLAG-WAVING BURGERS

The meat is red, the buns are white, and the blue? It's inside the burger, so it doesn't stick to the grill or ooze out before you bite in!

1 to 1½ pounds ground beef or ground turkey (see note)

½ cup crumbled blue cheese

4 hamburger buns

salt and pepper

GARNISHES AND CONDIMENT SUGGESTIONS:
mayonnaise, mustard, ketchup or barbecue sauce, lettuce, sliced tomatoes, sweet onions (such as Walla Walla or Vidalia), and roasted piquillo peppers, cut into strips

DO AHEAD *(burger patties can be assembled ahead and refrigerated)*

Season the ground meat with salt and pepper. Divide the meat into four equal portions. Make two patties from each portion of the meat (for a total of eight). Place one quarter of the crumbled blue cheese in the center of four patties, and then top with the remaining patties to form four burgers. Crimp the edges with your fingers to seal the cheese in the center. Grill or pan-fry the burger patties to desired degree of doneness. Garnish each burger as desired.

Prep Time: 10 minutes
Cooking Time: 15 minutes

If you use turkey, you might want to mix a raw egg into the meat. Sometimes ground turkey can be a little crumbly for a burger.

GRILLED GINGER-PEACHES

Folks love the idea of dessert from the grill. Let the peaches get some grill marks, and they're ready for their mascarpone dollop. The gingery crumbs add flavor and crunch. This is yummy with plums, too.

2 perfectly ripe peaches

about a tablespoonful of butter, melted (with a splash of rum, if desired)

3 Triple Ginger Snaps

4 tablespoons mascarpone

drizzle of honey

VEGETARIAN

Preheat grill to medium heat. Halve the peaches, removing the pit. Brush the cut sides with a little melted butter. Grill the peaches, cut side down, until marked and warm. Crush the ginger snaps into small crumbs. Sweeten the mascarpone to taste with honey, and spoon about a tablespoon into each peach hollow. Top with cookie crumbs and drizzle with more honey, if desired.

Prep Time: 10 minutes
Cooking Time: 5 minutes

RED, WHITE, and BLUEBERRY SMOOTHIE

The tart and tangy frozen yogurt craze swept the West Coast a while back. TJ's heard the buzz and provided a much less spendy alternative to the boutique yogurt shops' pricey offerings. Of course, you can make these treats with fresh berries and non-frozen yogurt—just add a handful of ice cubes to chill things out.

FOR EACH DRINK:

1 cup frozen blueberries

1 cup plain nonfat frozen yogurt

½ cup milk

squeeze of honey or Trader Joe's Organic Blue Agave Syrup

handful of strawberries and/or raspberries, for garnish

Blend all ingredients (except berries for garnish) in blender. Pour into tall glass.

. . . .

I like this with the red berries as garnish, but you can blend them in, too!

. . . .

FRENCH FÊTE

- GOUGERES
- SALADE VERTE
- PORK WITH MUSTARD CRÈME SAUCE
- MOCHA POTS DE CRÈME
- FRENCH 75

Berets and mustaches for everyone! A French evening is fun and elegant, and doesn't have to be *beaucoup* work. The *gougeres* ("goo-zjairz") can be made ahead and frozen, and the pots de crème can be done the day before, too. If you need an extra something to go with your pork, a simple potato gratin is a classically delicious (and *très Français*) addition to this meal.

GOUGERES

Perfect with a glass of wine, n'est-ce pas?

4 tablespoons butter

¼ cup milk

¼ cup water

½ cup flour

2 large eggs,
at room temperature

¾ cup Trader Joe's Swiss and
Gruyère Shredded Cheese Blend

DO AHEAD *(can bake and freeze)*
VEGETARIAN

Preheat oven to 400°F. In a medium saucepan, combine butter, milk, and water and bring to a simmer. When butter is melted, add all the flour at one time. Stir with a wooden spoon until a paste forms. Cook 2 to 3 minutes, stirring, until the dough pulls away from the side of the pan and a film appears on the bottom of the pan. Cool to room temperature, about 5 minutes. Add one egg, then beat with a wooden spoon or a mixer until the egg is incorporated. (At first, the dough will look "separated," but as you mix it, the egg will become incorporated and the dough will look smooth and satiny.) Add the remaining egg and repeat the process. Add the cheese and stir to incorporate.

Spoon or pipe tablespoon-sized dollops of dough onto a parchment-lined baking sheet. If you want the gougeres to be shiny, brush them with egg wash made from an egg and a bit of water. Bake until golden and fragrant, about 20 minutes.

Prep Time: 10 minutes
Cooking Time: 20 minutes

Gougeres freeze beautifully and can be reheated from frozen in less than 10 minutes.

SALADE VERTE

I love this salad made with mâche, but it's great with other tender greens, too. If it's just me, I make it with everything tossed in, but if I'm serving guests, I usually keep the nuts, bacon, and cheese in little bowls on the side so folks can serve themselves according to their diets and preferences— as long as they leave some bacon and blue for me!

4 strips good-quality bacon, cut into small pieces

6 ounces soft-leafed lettuce, such as mâche or butter lettuce, or Trader Joe's Baby Spring Mix

½ green apple, skin on

2 ounces Roquefort cheese, crumbled

¼ cup toasted walnuts, coarsely chopped

VINAIGRETTE:

2 tablespoons red wine vinegar

1 tablespoon Dijon mustard

2 tablespoons olive oil

4 tablespoons canola oil

salt and pepper

Sauté the bacon pieces until crisp. Drain on paper towels. Assemble the salad by arranging a bed of lettuce either on a platter or individual plates. Cut the apple into matchsticks. Arrange the bacon, Roquefort, apple matchsticks, and walnuts atop the lettuce.

FOR VINAIGRETTE: Whisk together the vinegar and mustard. Slowly drizzle in a little of the olive oil, whisking constantly. Continue to add the olive oil and the canola oil as you whisk, until the oil is incorporated. Taste the vinaigrette and adjust seasoning with salt and pepper. Drizzle lightly over the composed salad.

Prep Time: 10 minutes

Cooking Time: 5 minutes

To cut the matchsticks, cut the apple in half, stem to blossom end. Lay the apple, cut side down, on the cutting board. Cut the apple into thin slices, skipping over the core section. Then stack up a few of those slices, and cut those thinly into sticks. Repeat with the rest of the slices. Do this right before you serve the salad so the apples don't turn brown. If you need to cut them ahead of time, pop the matchsticks into a bowl of water with some lemon juice squeezed in. Drain well before adding to the salad.

PORK *with* MUSTARD CRÈME SAUCE

This is a great weeknight dinner because it goes together quickly and tastes great, but it's also fancy enough for guests. Don't you love recipes you can dress up or down, depending upon the situation? "Little Black Dress Recipes"—hmmm...There might be a cookbook in that!

1 pound pork tenderloin

3 tablespoons butter

1 shallot, minced

½ cup dry white wine

½ cup chicken broth

½ cup crème fraîche
or heavy cream

2 tablespoons Dijon mustard

salt and pepper

chopped fresh chives,
for garnish

GLUTEN-FREE

Preheat oven to 400°F. Season pork tenderloin with salt and pepper. In a medium sauté pan, heat the butter until melted and brown the pork on all sides. Remove pork to an ovensafe dish and roast until cooked through (the internal temperature should be 150°F), 12 to 15 minutes. While the pork roasts, add the shallot to the sauté pan and sauté until fragrant, 2 to 3 minutes. Add the wine and chicken broth and bring to a boil. Simmer until reduced by half, about 3 minutes. Add the crème fraîche and mustard and simmer to warm through. When pork is cooked, let stand 5 minutes, then slice. Add any accumulated juices to the sauce and adjust seasoning to taste with salt and pepper. Pour sauce over pork slices and garnish with chopped chives.

Prep Time: 5 minutes
Cooking Time: 25 minutes

MOCHA POTS DE CRÈME

Elegant, delicious, and individual—just right for a party! These pretty little pots of creamy goodness aren't too, too sweet—they're the perfect finish to a French soirée.

½ cup cream

½ cup milk

1 teaspoon instant coffee granules

3 ounces bittersweet chocolate, chopped

3 egg yolks

2 tablespoons granulated sugar, divided

pinch salt

¼ cup crème fraîche

chocolate-covered espresso beans

DO AHEAD
VEGETARIAN, GLUTEN-FREE

Preheat oven to 325°F. In a small saucepan, heat the cream and milk to a simmer. Stir in the instant coffee granules. Place the chopped chocolate in a heatproof bowl and pour the hot cream mixture over it. Let stand 1 to 2 minutes and stir to combine and melt the chocolate. In another bowl, whisk together the egg yolks, 1 tablespoon sugar, and salt. Pour about ½ cup of the chocolate mixture into the yolks and stir to combine well. Add this mixture back into the rest of the chocolate mixture and stir to combine. Place four 4-ounce ramekins in a casserole dish and divide the chocolate mixture evenly among the ramekins. Place the casserole dish in the oven, then pour in enough hot water to come halfway up the sides of the ramekins. Bake until there is just a slight jiggle in the center of the custard, about 30 minutes. Carefully remove the casserole from the oven, and then remove the ramekins from the water. Let cool slightly before refrigerating. Chill at least 2 hours before serving.

To serve, whisk together the crème fraîche and remaining 1 tablespoon sugar. (Add more sugar if you have a sweet tooth!) Garnish each pot de crème with a dollop of the sweetened crème fraîche and top with a chocolate-covered espresso bean.

Prep Time: 20 minutes
Cooking Time: 30 minutes

FRENCH 75

This classic beverage packs a wallop, as did the World war Two French field artillery guns it's named for.

FOR EACH DRINK:

1 ounce Bombay Sapphire gin

1 teaspoon sugar

2 teaspoons lemon juice

⅓ cup champagne

Add the gin, sugar, and lemon juice to a cocktail shaker full of ice. Shake, strain into a cocktail glass, and top with champagne.

GRAB & GO
No-Prep French Fête

It's as easy as *un*, *deux*, *trois* to fill a cart with delicious, French-inspired delicacies for an impromptu soirée. From the frozen section:

- **FRENCH ONION SOUP**
- **CHEESE SOUFFLÉ**
- **TARTE D'ALSACE**
- **QUICHE**
- **CHOCOLATE CRÈME BRÛLÉE**
- **MACARONS**

POOL PARTY

- SMOKED TROUT PEPPER SPREAD
- WATERMELON, FETA, AND OLIVE SALAD
- CONFETTI PASTA SALAD
- GRILLED ARTICHOKE PESTO AND GOAT CHEESE PIZZA
- BEER CAN CHICKEN
- MINTY PINEAPPLE LICUADO
- BLUEBERRY GINGER-CRUMBLE PIE

Whether you're lounging beside your fabulous backyard water oasis or dipping your toes in an inflatable baby pool, keep cool with this low-stress, big-flavor menu. The spreads and dessert can be made ahead, the pizzas can be tossed on the grill as soon as it's hot, and the Beer Can Chicken can hang out while you judge the cannonball contest.

SMOKED TROUT PEPPER SPREAD

The romaine leaves add a cool crunch and look just gorgeous on a platter, but crackers are a great delivery system for this spread, too!

2 (3.9-ounce) tins Smoked Trout in Canola Oil, drained

4 piquillo peppers

½ cup walnuts

4 tablespoons butter, at room temperature

juice of half a lemon

salt and pepper

romaine heart leaves

DO AHEAD
GLUTEN-FREE

In a food processor, combine the drained trout, peppers, walnuts, and butter and pulse to combine. Season to taste with lemon juice, salt, and pepper. Chill 20 minutes to allow flavors to meld. Spoon dollops of the spread into romaine leaves to serve.

Prep Time: 5 minutes

WATERMELON, FETA, and OLIVE SALAD

I know this combo sounds crazy, but get ready for a wild explosion of sweet, salty, juicy, bright goodness!

2 cups cubed watermelon

⅓ cup crumbled feta cheese

½ cup pitted black olives

1 tablespoon red wine vinegar

3 tablespoons olive oil

¼ cup chopped fresh mint

DO AHEAD
VEGETARIAN, GLUTEN-FREE

Toss all ingredients together to combine. Serve in a glass bowl or hollowed-out watermelon shell.

Prep Time: 10 minutes

CONFETTI PASTA SALAD

The colors pop on the platter, and the flavors pop in your mouth!

1 (16-ounce) bag farfalle

1 (7-ounce) container Trader Giotto's Pesto alla Genovese (in the refrigerated case)

½ (13.75-ounce) jar Trader Joe's Corn and Chile Tomato-Less Salsa

1 cup Trader Joe's Mixed Medley Cherry Tomatoes, cut in half

1 cup Ciliegini mozzarella balls, cut in half

salt and pepper

**DO AHEAD
VEGETARIAN**

Cook the pasta in a large pot of rapidly boiling salted water until al dente. Drain and rinse under cold running water. In a large bowl, combine the pasta, pesto, corn salsa, cherry tomatoes, and mozzarella balls. Toss to combine, and adjust seasoning to taste.

Prep Time: 10 minutes
Cooking Time: 12 minutes

GRILLED ARTICHOKE PESTO *and* GOAT CHEESE PIZZA

People are really impressed with pizza made on the grill. I don't oil the dough or the grill grates—I find that if the grates are clean and hot, the dough won't stick.

1 pound pizza dough

½ (12-ounce) jar Trader Giotto's Artichoke Pesto (or another pesto or spread)

2 ounces goat cheese (Trader Joe's Chèvre, Silver Goat Chèvre, or Madame Chèvre)

VEGETARIAN

Preheat grill to medium. Form the dough into a large flattened rectangle. Place the dough on the grill and cook about 4 minutes, until grill marks form and dough looks cooked on the bottom. Flip and cook on the other side about 2 to 3 more minutes. If the dough puffs too much, pierce it with a skewer or knife. When the dough is nearly cooked through, spread pesto on the pizza and top with dollops of goat cheese. Close the grill lid and cook about 2 minutes, until pesto and cheese are warm.

Prep Time: 10 minutes
Cooking Time: 10 minutes

BEER CAN CHICKEN

Not a new idea, but just plain fun for pool parties or any grilling event. I'm sure you'll find something to do with the other half of that beer!

1 (12-ounce) can beer, with half the beer "removed"

1 (3- to 4-pound) whole chicken

Trader Joe's Everyday Seasoning or another spice blend (or salt and pepper)

Heat the grill or coals to high. Using the indirect-heat method, either turn one side of the grill off or mound the coals on one side of the grill. Rub the chicken inside and out with the Everyday Seasoning spice blend or salt and pepper, and set it on top of the beer can. Balance the can and the chicken (using the legs and can as a tripod) on the indirect side of the heat (over the burner that is off, or where there are no coals). Close the grill lid and cook the chicken 40 minutes. Using tongs, rotate the chicken so that the side that was farthest from the heat source is now the closest. Close lid and cook another 30 minutes, or until the joints are loose, the skin is crisp, and the juices run clear. Carefully remove the chicken and the beer can from the grill, and remove the beer can from the chicken. The beer remaining in the can will be very hot—use tongs and/or hot pads for this. Let the chicken rest 10 minutes before carving.

Prep Time: 5 minutes
Cooking Time: 45 to 55 minutes

• •
You can use fruit juice cans, soda, or any other canned beverage you like for this—the size of the can is important for balance, so if you need to, pour the liquid into a can tall enough to support the chicken—a 12-ounce beer can usually does the trick. Of course, if you substitute another beverage, you'll need to rename the dish!
• •

MINTY PINEAPPLE LICUADO

As summery as a cannonball, this minty, pineappley refresher is great with or without vodka.

FOR EACH DRINK:

1 cup fresh pineapple cubes

about 5 mint leaves

squeeze of lime juice

handful of crushed ice

1 tablespoon simple syrup, Trader Joe's Organic Blue Agave Syrup, or honey

sparkling water

Place the pineapple, mint, lime juice, crushed ice, and simple syrup, agave, or honey in a blender. Blend until smooth, adding a splash of water if necessary to facilitate blending. Once blended, add sparkling water to desired state of fizziness. (Add a splash of vodka for grown-ups who aren't on lifeguard duty.)

BLUEBERRY GINGER-CRUMBLE PIE

I love what ginger does for berries, especially blueberries. It brightens the flavor in a special way—puts a skip in their step, somehow. Try some in plain yogurt with berries, and see if you don't agree!

2 pints blueberries

1 tablespoon flour

¾ cup sugar

pinch salt

zest of 1 lemon

1 Trader Joe's Gourmet Pie Crust (in the frozen-food section), defrosted (refreeze the remaining one for another use)

1 tablespoon butter

CRUMBLE TOPPING:

2 cups flour

1 cup firmly packed brown sugar

8 ounces cold butter, cut into chunks

3 tablespoons chopped candied ginger

pinch salt

**DO AHEAD
VEGETARIAN**

Preheat oven to 425°F. Combine berries, flour, sugar, salt, and lemon zest. Roll out pie dough and fit into pie pan. Fill with berry mixture. Dot with butter.

FOR CRUMBLE TOPPING: In a mixing bowl or food processor, combine ingredients to a crumbly texture. (If using a mixing bowl, use your fingers, a wire pastry blender, or two butter knives.) Press onto top of pie filling. Place the pie pan on a baking sheet and bake 10 minutes. Reduce heat to 350°F and bake 40 to 50 minutes, until filling is bubbling and crumble topping is golden. Cool before serving.

Prep Time: 15 minutes
Cooking Time: 1 hour

GIRLS' NIGHT IN

- **RAPUNZEL SALAD**
- **MEDITERRANEAN TURKEY SLIDERS**
- **BANABERRIES WITH TOBLERONE SAUCE**
- **CHEZ CHERIE COCKTAIL**

A night with the girls can fix a host of problems. We need our girlfriends, and this menu will keep them close! Pretty, tasty, and fun—just like my BFFs.

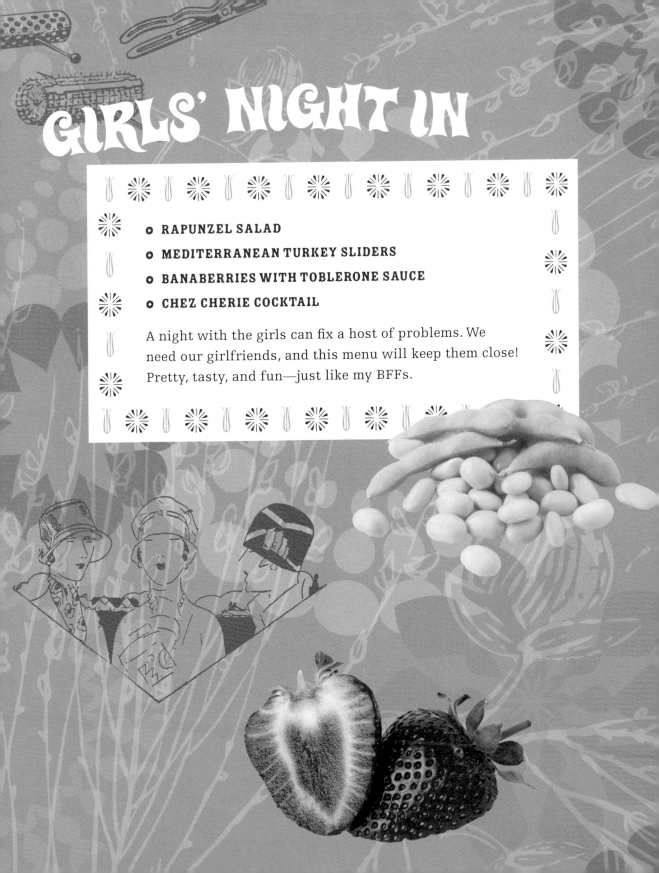

RAPUNZEL SALAD

Remember the fairy tale about "Rapunzel, Rapunzel, let down your golden hair"? She was a pregnant girl who craved her greens—and I recently read that those greens were believed to be mâche. They're my favorite salad greens, so I might make a deal with the devil for a supply, too. The cute little clusters of soft, nutty leaves make a salad so pretty.

1 (4-ounce) bag mâche lettuce

⅓ (10-ounce) bag shredded green cabbage

handful of shredded carrots

2 handfuls of shelled edamame

2 tablespoons seasoned rice vinegar

2 teaspoons Trader Joe's Organic Blue Agave Syrup

6 tablespoons grapeseed or canola oil

salt and pepper

VEGAN, GLUTEN-FREE

In a large bowl, toss together the mâche, cabbage, carrots, and edamame. In a small bowl, whisk together the rice vinegar and agave syrup. While whisking, stream in the oil until the dressing is well combined. Season to taste with salt and pepper, and lightly dress the salad just before serving.

Prep Time: 10 minutes

MEDITERRANEAN TURKEY SLIDERS

Seriously—what is it about us women and teeny food? We seem to love the Barbie-sized proportions of sliders and other "mini" creations (mini cupcakes, anyone?). I know we aren't fooling ourselves when we eat more than a doll-sized portion of these sliders, but I have to admit that I fall for them every time!

1 pound ground turkey

3 tablespoons Trader Joe's Traditional Olive Tapenade

3 tablespoons crumbled feta cheese

salt and pepper

1 tablespoon olive oil

8 (1 package) mini hamburger buns

whole grain Dijon mustard

¼ red onion, thinly sliced

3 cornichons, sliced in half lengthwise

DO AHEAD (form patties)

In a bowl, combine the ground turkey, olive tapenade, and feta. Season generously with salt and pepper. Form into patties a little bit larger than the buns. Over medium heat, heat the oil in a medium skillet or grill pan. Cook the turkey patties about 4 minutes on one side, flip, and cook until cooked through, about 3 minutes on the other side. Remove to a platter, and in the same pan, toast the buns briefly. Build the sliders by spreading a little mustard on one side of each bun, topping it with a turkey patty, and garnishing with a few slivers of red onion and a cornichon slice or two.

Prep Time: 15 minutes
Cooking Time: 15 minutes

I like to use ground turkey that has about 24 percent fat content, so I avoid the all-white-meat ground turkey. It's just too dry to be delicious. I've also used the refrigerated Traditional Olive Tapenade in this recipe, rather than the shelf-stable Trader Joe's Green Olive Tapenade, because of the higher oil content. Not a lot of oil goes into these burgers, but the little bit that does helps make the sliders tender and tasty.

BANABERRIES with TOBLERONE SAUCE

There's more fruit than chocolate in this dessert—so it's health food, right? If you made it with dark chocolate instead of Toblerone, it definitely would be medicine!

⅔ cup cream

1 (3.52-ounce) bar Toblerone (or another good chocolate bar), chopped

1 tablespoon liqueur, optional (Frangelico or Amaretto would be delish!)

1 ripe banana, thinly sliced

1 pint strawberries, raspberries, or a combination

DO AHEAD
VEGETARIAN, GLUTEN-FREE

In a small sauté pan, heat cream to a simmer. Remove it from the heat and stir in the chopped chocolate. Let stand for a minute or two to let the heat of the cream melt the chocolate, and stir until well combined and smooth. Stir in liqueur, if using. Set aside (in the saucepan, to keep it warm). Divide the berries into small bowls and dollop some of the sauce on top of each one.

Prep Time: 5 minutes
Cooking Time: 5 minutes

CHEZ CHERIE COCKTAIL

I came up with this pretty-in-pink punch one sunny afternoon, and I love the fizzy, frothy look and taste of it. I think you'll agree that it's a great, girly sipper. It's also good with half lemonade, half champagne!

FOR EACH DRINK:

1 scoop raspberry sorbet

Trader Joe's French Market Sparkling Pink Lemonade

splash vodka

raspberries, for garnish

Place the raspberry sorbet in a tall cocktail glass. Pour pink lemonade into the glass until it's about ¾ full. Add a splash of vodka and stir gently to combine. Garnish with a few raspberries, if desired.

PASSAGE TO INDIA

- CACHUMBER
- BUTTERNUT SQUASH AND GREEN BEAN CURRY
- MANGO-GINGER CHUTNEY-GLAZED CHICKEN
- PASSAGE TO INDIA PORK
- CHAI AND BISCUITS
- MANGO LASSI

Whether you're donning saris and reclining on rose petals or simply renting some Bollywood classics, this menu will put you in the proper frame of mind and palate.

CACHUMBER

The refreshingly chilly crunch of this salad is a great accompaniment to hot, spicy foods. It's also good with some plain yogurt in a pita.

2 ripe tomatoes, seeded and chopped

1 cup chopped onion

¼ cup chopped cilantro

1 to 2 tablespoons minced jalapeño, or to taste

juice of 1 lemon

salt, sugar, and pepper, to taste

DO AHEAD
VEGAN, GLUTEN-FREE

Toss all ingredients together and let stand 30 minutes, to let flavors meld. Taste and adjust seasonings.

Prep Time: 5 minutes, plus 30 minutes for flavor melding

GRAB & GO
No-Prep Passage to India

In the past few years, TJ's has upped their game on Indian offerings. Lots of great choices await you in the frozen aisle and the sauce shelves.

- **CURRY OR MASALA SIMMER SAUCE**

From the frozen section:

- **PANEER TIKKA MASALA WITH SPINACH CURRY**
- **CURRIED LENTILS AND CUMIN-FLAVORED RICE**
- **GARLIC NAAN**
- **VEGETABLE SAMOSAS**

BUTTERNUT SQUASH and GREEN BEAN CURRY

 There's great color and flavor in this vegetarian entrée that can also be served as a side dish. The coconut milk–braised vegetables are tender and tasty, while the chiles and cashews bring heat and crunch to the table. Great served with steamed white or brown rice.

8 ounces butternut squash cubes, steamed, microwaved, or roasted until just tender

2 cups frozen haricots verts (French green beans)

1 cup coconut milk

2 teaspoons curry powder

½ (4-ounce can) Hatch Valley Fire-Roasted Diced Green Chiles

salt and pepper

2 tablespoons chopped cashews, for garnish

DO AHEAD
VEGAN, GLUTEN-FREE

Place the butternut squash and green beans in a sauté pan and add coconut milk. Bring to a simmer and cook until vegetables are tender, 10 to 12 minutes. Stir in curry powder and chiles and simmer another 2 to 3 minutes. Adjust seasoning to taste and garnish with chopped cashews.

Prep Time: 10 minutes
Cooking Time: 20 minutes

MANGO-GINGER CHUTNEY-GLAZED CHICKEN

This chicken is the base for a great salad—cut it into strips and serve it atop a bed of spinach. Add a handful of dried cranberries, or TJ's Golden Berry Blend, if you like. Some toasted chopped nuts would be fab, too!

4 boneless, skinless chicken breasts (about 1½ pounds)

pinch of ground cumin

2 teaspoons ground Trader Joe's Everyday Seasoning

3 tablespoons olive oil, divided

½ red onion, thinly sliced

3 cubes frozen garlic

½ (9-ounce) jar Trader Joe's Mango Ginger Chutney

2 tablespoons Dijon mustard

1 tablespoon red wine vinegar

salt and pepper

DO AHEAD *(warm in low oven or microwave)*
GLUTEN-FREE

Place the chicken breasts between two sheets of parchment and use a meat mallet (or the bottom of a skillet) to pound the chicken breasts until they're about ¼-inch thick. Season with cumin and Everyday Seasoning. Drizzle about 2 teaspoons of the olive oil into a grill pan or sauté pan, and, working in batches, cook the chicken about 3 minutes per side, until cooked through. Remove to a warm platter and repeat until all chicken is cooked. Add a splash more oil, if needed, and sauté the red onion for 2 to 3 minutes. Add the garlic and sauté until fragrant, 1 to 2 minutes. Place the onions and garlic on the chicken. In a bowl, stir together the chutney, mustard, and vinegar, and whisk in the remaining oil. Season to taste with a little more Everyday Seasoning. Spoon over chicken breasts and serve.

Prep Time: 10 minutes
Cooking Time: 20 minutes

PASSAGE TO INDIA PORK

In recent years, TJ's saag paneer, masala simmer sauces, and naan have found their places on the shelves, with great customer approval. It's fun to try new flavor combinations, and TJ's makes it so easy to travel the world's flavor map.

1 (¾ to 1 pound) pork tenderloin

1 tablespoon olive oil

1 (10.5-ounce) package Trader Joe's Indian Fare Dal Makhani

salt and pepper

DO AHEAD *(warm in low oven or microwave)*
GLUTEN-FREE

Preheat oven to 400°F. Season tenderloin with salt and pepper. In a large sauté pan, heat the oil and sear the tenderloin on all sides. Place in the preheated oven and roast until cooked through, about 15 minutes (the internal temperature should be 145 to 150°F). Remove pork to a cutting board and let rest 5 minutes before cutting into ½-inch slices. While pork rests, heat the contents of the dal makhani package in the same sauté pan. Arrange pork slices on serving plate and pour sauce over them. Serve with rice or polenta to sop up every bit of sauce.

Prep Time: 5 minutes
Cooking Time: 20 minutes

Once again, my hairdresser comes to the rescue. Thanks, Christine, for letting me know about this yummy Dal Makhani stuff!

CHAI *and* BISCUITS

Would it be wrong to use the crunchy Almondina cookies in lieu of spoons? How wrong, on a scale of 1 to 10?

2 cups milk

1 (3.39-ounce) package instant vanilla pudding mix

2 tablespoons Trader Joe's Spicy Chai Latte mix

1 (4-ounce) package Almondina Chocolate Cherry Biscuits

DO AHEAD
VEGETARIAN

Pour milk into a medium bowl. Whisk in the vanilla pudding mix and Spicy Chai mix. Chill. Serve with biscuits.

Prep Time: 5 minutes

MANGO LASSI

A milkshake with a little Indian flair...I wonder how this would taste with a little citrus vodka stirred in? Hmmm...BRB!

FOR EACH DRINK:

1 mango, diced (or about a cup of frozen cubes)

½ cup plain or vanilla yogurt

1 teaspoon vanilla

2 tablespoons sugar, divided

1 cup milk

handful of ice cubes (if using fresh mango), optional

DO AHEAD
VEGETARIAN, GLUTEN-FREE
(if gluten-free yogurt is used)

Put the mango cubes and yogurt in a blender and whirl to combine. Add the vanilla, 1 tablespoon of the sugar, and the milk. Whirl again and taste. Add more sugar if desired (the sweetness of mangoes varies according to type and season). Add the ice cubes, if desired, and whirl until smooth.

Prep Time: 5 minutes

This recipe makes one large serving. For a smaller drink, divide the ingredients in half.

HALLOWEEN

- VAMPIRE-REPELLENT BEEF GOULASH
- SIMPLE, SLURPABLE PUMPKIN SOUP
- DAY OF THE DEAD BONES AND GORE-Y DIP
- PUMPKIN PIE MARTINI

Before the kids go candy-crazy, it's a good idea to get something in their tummies that's not sugar-based! Soup is satisfying and filling, especially if the weather is suitably dreary. (In Southern California, we often have what I call "bikini Halloween" weather, which ruins the spooky mood somehow.)

VAMPIRE-REPELLENT BEEF GOULASH

Garlic and red wine make a fragrant base for this seasonally appropriate stew. The orange butternut squash is the perfect color for the evening, and the olives, well, besides the briny flavor they bring, those are the eyeballs, of course! Ya gotta have a little Halloween gross-out!

1 tablespoon olive oil

1 pound lean beef stew meat

1 onion, chopped

6 cubes frozen garlic

1½ cups red wine

1 cup beef broth

1 (12-ounce) bag butternut squash cubes

1 cup green olives stuffed with pimento

salt and pepper

DO AHEAD
GLUTEN-FREE

In a large saucepan, heat the oil and, working in batches, sauté the stew meat until well browned. As each batch is browned, remove to a platter and continue until all meat is browned. In the same pan, sauté the onion until softened and fragrant, 3 to 4 minutes. Add the garlic and sauté until fragrant, 2 to 3 minutes. Add the wine, bring to a boil, reduce the heat, and simmer until reduced by half, 4 to 5 minutes. Add the beef broth and meat to the pan. Bring to a boil, reduce the heat, cover, and simmer 30 minutes. Add the butternut squash cubes, season lightly with salt and pepper, and simmer, covered, another 15 to 20 minutes. Add the olives and warm through.

Prep Time: 5 minutes
Cooking Time: 1 hour

••

You could hollow out a pumpkin to use as a tureen for this stew. But be sure to serve it with something soppable—mashed potatoes, buttered noodles, or couscous. You'll want to catch every drop of the delicious sauce!

••

SIMPLE, SLURPABLE PUMPKIN SOUP

Sadly, you can't really use jack-o'-lanterns for cooking. Those babies are bred for carving, not cooking, and the flesh is sadly stringy. But the TJ's canned pumpkin is great stuff, and worth hoarding. During the Great Pumpkin Shortage of '09, I stockpiled cans galore and was able to dole them out to friends who'd gotten caught short, making me their kitchen hero!

2 teaspoons olive oil

½ (4-ounce) package cubed Italian-Style Bacon Pancetta

3 tablespoons chopped onions, garlic, and shallot combination

1 (15-ounce) can Organic Pumpkin Purée

2 cups chicken or vegetable broth

2 tablespoons dry sherry (optional)

1½ cups Trader Joe's Swiss and Gruyère Shredded Cheese Blend

salt, pepper, and red chile pepper flakes

**DO AHEAD
GLUTEN-FREE**

In a saucepan, heat the olive oil and sauté the pancetta until browned. Remove with a slotted spoon and set aside. In the same pan, sauté the onion and shallots until fragrant, 2 to 3 minutes. Add the pumpkin purée and broth. Bring to a boil, reduce the heat, and simmer 10 minutes. Add the sherry (if using), and warm through. Turn off the heat and stir in the shredded cheese to melt. Adjust seasoning with salt, pepper, and red chile pepper flakes. Garnish with reserved pancetta.

Prep Time: 5 minutes
Cooking Time: 15 minutes

In the TJ's refrigerated produce section, there's a little plastic box with a combination of chopped onions and shallots. If you're super prone to tears when chopping, these might be a boon to your kitchen enjoyment. If chopping is a Zen exercise for you (as it is for me), give your knife skills a workout. You can use just shallot, onion, or a combination—whatever's handy!

DAY of the DEAD BONES and GORE-Y DIP

I think it was a Halloween issue of Martha Stewart Living *where I first saw this idea for bone-shaped meringues—Martha loves her some Halloween! The blood-red dipping sauce adds a ghoulish touch, which adds to the fun.*

3 egg whites

¾ cup granulated sugar

½ teaspoon vanilla

pinch of cinnamon

SAUCE:

1 (12-ounce) bag frozen raspberries

½ cup sugar

juice of ½ lemon

DO AHEAD
VEGETARIAN, GLUTEN-FREE

Preheat oven to 250°F. With an electric mixer, whip the egg whites until foamy. Continue to beat, sprinkling the sugar in gradually, until all sugar is added and whites are stiff and glossy. Add the vanilla and cinnamon and whip to combine. Line a baking sheet with parchment and, using a piping bag with a round tip or a resealable plastic bag with one corner snipped out, pipe the meringue mixture into bone shapes, 4 to 5 inches long. Bake until meringue is set, about 45 minutes.

FOR SAUCE: In a medium saucepan, bring the mixture to a boil, reduce the heat, and simmer about 10 minutes, until syrupy. (At this point, you can strain the mixture if you want, but I think the seeds add to the gorey look!) Cool to room temperature. Purée the mixture in a food processor or blender. Adjust flavor with a little more lemon juice if desired. Don't worry if the sauce isn't ultrasweet—the bones will be! Use the sauce as a drizzle, or pour into bowls for bone-dipping.

Prep Time: 20 minutes
Cooking Time: 45 minutes

I like to scoop some coffee or vanilla ice cream, crisscross a couple meringue bones over the top, and garnish with a drizzle of the sauce.

PUMPKIN PIE MARTINI

I saw a version of this cocktail on a recipe card at the fabulous Surfas restaurant supply store in Culver City, California. Props to Executive Chef Brandi Quinn for inspiring this TJ's version, which makes for a very happy Halloween, indeed!

FOR EACH DRINK:

butter, at room temperature, for glass rim

Triple Ginger Snaps, crushed, for glass rim

2 tablespoons Trader Joe's Pumpkin Butter

4 tablespoons vodka

splash of cream

Rub the rim of a martini glass with a tiny bit of room-temperature butter. Dip into gingersnap crumbs. In a cocktail shaker with ice, shake pumpkin butter, vodka, and cream. Strain into prepared glass.

TAILGATING TREATS

- ○ **WASABI DEVILED EGGS**
- ○ **PULLED PORK PANINI**
- ○ **FLAVORS-OF-THE-MED SPREAD**
- ○ **CHERRY BROWNIE BITES**

In many parts of the country, tailgating is an art form. Here in Southern California, with cross-town rival college teams, the tailgating competition is as fierce as the on-field action. (My neighbor's tailgating rig is nicer than my kitchen!) This menu can hold its own, even with the big dogs, but you won't have to get up at the ugly side of morning in order to pull it off. Go, team!

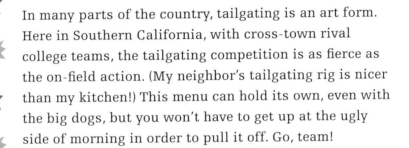

WASABI DEVILED EGGS

I've said it before, and I'll say it again: Deviled eggs may be old-school, but they always disappear fast off a party tray! The wasabi gives these a nice kick, and they come together quickly. If you're really pinched for time, TJ's sells already hard-boiled eggs.

6 hard-boiled eggs, peeled and cut in half

3 to 6 tablespoons Wasabi Mayonnaise (for less spice, use 3 tablespoons regular mayo and 3 tablespoons Wasabi Mayo)

3 green onions, minced

salt and pepper

DO AHEAD
VEGETARIAN, GLUTEN-FREE

Place the egg yolks in a small bowl and mash with a fork. Add the mayonnaise (wasabi and/or regular) and most of the minced green onions. Stir to combine and season to taste with salt and pepper. Spoon or pipe the filling back into the egg whites, and garnish with the reserved minced green onion.

Prep Time: 10 minutes

GRAB & GO
Mix and Match Beers

Beer is the order of the day for tailgaters, so go with something that fits the persona of your favorite team—the Internet is rife with suggestions around game time—or stick with the tried and true: TJ's has a wall of beers, so mix and match or stick with your favorite kind.

PULLED PORK PANINI

These go together nearly as fast as my family can gobble them. The creamy, cold crunch of the coleslaw is great with the sweet, smoky pork. Yum!

4 panini rustic rolls

1 (16-ounce) package Trader Joe's Pulled Pork in Smoky BBQ Sauce

½ (10-ounce) bag shredded cabbage

handful of shredded carrots

½ cup organic mayonnaise

2 tablespoons red wine vinegar

salt and pepper

Split the rolls horizontally and toast. Heat pork according to package directions and divide among rolls. Combine cabbage and carrots. Stir together mayonnaise and vinegar. Toss cabbage and carrots with dressing. Season to taste with salt and pepper. Serve slaw in sandwiches or on the side.

Prep Time: 10 minutes
Cooking Time: 5 minutes

FLAVORS-OF-THE-MED SPREAD

Warning—this stuff is seriously addictive. It goes together very quickly, and there are a bunch of terrific uses for it. It's pretty garlic-intense, so make sure everybody eats some!

½ (4-ounce) can Hatch Valley Diced Green Chiles

6 cloves garlic

1 tablespoon capers, drained

¾ cup (about 4 ounces) crumbled feta cheese

½ cup organic mayonnaise

¼ cup crème fraîche

1 teaspoon dried oregano

dash of Trader Joe's Chili Pepper Hot Sauce or Jalapeño Pepper Hot Sauce

DO AHEAD
VEGETARIAN, GLUTEN-FREE

Place the chiles, garlic, and capers in the bowl of a food processor and pulse until coarsely chopped. Add the feta, mayonnaise, crème fraîche, and oregano, and pulse until well combined. Add hot sauce to taste.

Prep Time: 10 minutes

Use as a spread on crostini or to make a version of garlic bread (spread on split baguettes and bake until warm). Also delicious as a dip with pita crisps or on panini.

CHERRY BROWNIE BITES

The cupcake format makes these easy to transport, and the cherries are a great little surprise. You could frost these with a little chocolate ganache (see note) and stick a cherry on top if you want to get fancy.

1 (16-ounce) box Trader Joe's Brownie Truffle Baking Mix

1 cup Trader Joe's Dark Morello Cherries in Light Syrup (jarred), drained

4 ounces butter, melted

2 eggs

**DO AHEAD
VEGETARIAN**

Preheat oven to 350°F. Line a muffin tin with paper liners. Place the brownie mix in a bowl and toss the cherries in the mix. Add the melted butter and stir to combine. Crack the eggs into a small bowl and whisk to combine, then add to brownie batter and combine well. Fill paper liners ⅔ full. Bake until a toothpick inserted into the center of a cupcake comes out clean, about 25 minutes.

Prep Time: 5 minutes
Cooking Time: 25 minutes

To make chocolate ganache, chop a cup of chocolate and put it into a heatproof bowl. Heat a cup of cream in a saucepan and pour over the chocolate. Let stand 5 minutes, then stir to evenly melt the chocolate. Cool. You can whip the ganache for a fluffier texture, or just spread it over the cupcakes.

AFTERNOON TEA

- **SMOKED SALMON ROSETTES WITH BASIL MAYONNAISE**
- **CHICKEN SALAD PINWHEELS**
- **GINGER CREAM SCONES**
- **LEMON HEAVEN SPREAD**
- **OOOH LA-LA BERRIES**

For a baby shower, a girlfriends' afternoon, or a mother-daughter day, afternoon tea is a great way to girl it up! This menu encourages you to crook your pinkie and sip for hours, with or without flowered dresses and hats. The vast array of blossoms available at TJ's can create a bower of floral wonder for your table.

SMOKED SALMON ROSETTES with BASIL MAYONNAISE

 Don't stress too much about getting the salmon to look like roses...a simple spiral roll is pretty, too! You'll have extra basil mayo spread—it's wonderful on tomato-mozzarella sandwiches, grilled fish or chicken, or in a chicken salad.

BASIL MAYONNAISE:

½ (4-ounce) package basil

3 (or more) cubes frozen garlic

1 cup organic mayonnaise

juice of ½ a lemon

salt and white pepper

TARTINES:

½ (18-ounce) package European-Style Whole Grain Bread, cut into rounds slightly larger than the cucumber rounds

salted butter, at room temperature

about 6 inches English cucumber, thinly sliced

¼ pound smoked salmon, thinly sliced

DO AHEAD

FOR BASIL MAYONNAISE: In a food processor with the motor running, drop basil leaves through the feeder tube and process until well chopped. Scrape down sides of bowl, add garlic, mayonnaise, and a squeeze of lemon juice, and process again. Taste and adjust seasonings, adding more lemon juice and some salt and white pepper, to taste.

FOR TARTINES: To assemble tartines, lightly butter one side of each bread round and place a cucumber slice in the center. Roll a strip of salmon into a spiral, and use your fingertips to gently roll the edges into a petal-like shape. Pipe or spoon a small dollop of basil mayonnaise on each cucumber slice and place a salmon "rose" on top.

Prep Time: 30 minutes

CHICKEN SALAD PINWHEELS

These look so pretty on a pastel platter, garnished with a few blossoms. You'll need an unsliced loaf of bread so that you can cut it yourself from end to end, rather than from top to bottom.

1 cup Trader Joe's Just Chicken (or other cooked chicken)

2 tablespoons chopped dried apricots (about 2)

2 ribs celery, chopped

2 tablespoons chopped pecans, toasted

2 tablespoons crème fraîche

2 tablespoons organic mayonnaise

salt and white pepper

1 loaf brioche or another good-quality white bread loaf, thinly sliced lengthwise, crusts removed

butter, at room temperature

DO AHEAD

Combine the chicken, dried apricots, celery, and pecans in a food processor and finely chop. Add the crème fraîche and mayonnaise, plus a little extra if the mixture seems dry. Season to taste with salt and white pepper.

Use a rolling pin to roll out the bread slices to make them a little larger and to compact the crumb a bit. Spread slices of bread with butter. Spread chicken mixture evenly over each slice, leaving one short end clean. Starting at the other short end, roll the sandwich moderately tightly, using the buttered end to seal the roll. Cut into pinwheel slices.

Prep Time: 20 minutes

GINGER CREAM SCONES

Scones are a tea menu requirement, if you ask me. You can switch this basic recipe up, using chopped dried apricots or dried cherries instead of or in addition to the candied ginger.

1 cup flour

1 teaspoon baking powder

2 tablespoons sugar

pinch salt

2 tablespoons butter

2 tablespoons chopped candied ginger

1 egg

¼ cup plus 1 tablespoon cream, divided

turbinado sugar, for garnish

DO AHEAD
VEGETARIAN

Preheat oven to 425°F. Combine the flour, baking powder, sugar, and salt in a medium bowl (or food processor). Mix in the butter (or pulse several times) until crumbly. Add chopped ginger, egg, and ¼ cup cream and mix just until combined. Turn the dough onto a floured surface and knead just until it comes together. Pat the dough out to 1- to 1½-inches thick and cut into triangles or circles. Place scones on a parchment-lined baking sheet and brush with remaining 1 tablespoon cream. Sprinkle with turbinado sugar and bake until golden, about 20 minutes. Serve with Lemon Heaven Spread.

Prep Time: 10 minutes
Cooking Time: 20 minutes

LEMON HEAVEN SPREAD

This may be the simplest recipe in the book, and also perhaps the most versatile—not to mention the most delicious! I've used this instead of pastry cream for a fruit tart, as a decadent filling for vanilla wafer sandwiches, to dip strawberries into, in a creamy trifle, on a strawberry pie instead of whipped cream, or as a midnight snack!

1 (10.5-ounce) jar Trader Joe's Lemon Curd

1 (8-ounce) container mascarpone

DO AHEAD
VEGETARIAN, GLUTEN-FREE

Stir together the lemon curd and mascarpone. Slather on scones.

Prep Time: 2 minutes

OOH-LA-LA BERRIES

In France, this is a familiar summer treat, but there they use soft brown sugar. I love the crunchy texture contrast of the turbinado sugar. Besides, it looks so sparkly in the bowl that it's just more festive!

1 (16-ounce) basket organic strawberries

1 (8-ounce) container crème fraîche

½ cup turbinado sugar

VEGETARIAN, GLUTEN-FREE

Rinse and pat the berries dry. Arrange on a platter. Place the crème fraîche and the turbinado sugar in separate bowls and nestle the bowls into the berries. Dip a berry into the crème fraîche and then into the sugar. Eat. Repeat.

Prep Time: 5 minutes

I've specified organic strawberries after reading a list of "The Dirty Dozen and the Clean Fifteen." Strawberries are apparently among the fruits that absorb any pesticides more readily, so I choose organic when I berry shop.

GRAB & GO
No-Prep Afternoon Tea

There are dozens of treats that would be great for a tea-time "emergency": Madeleines with lemon curd, lavosh (spread with cream cheese and a tapenade, then roll and slice), fab frozen French *macarons*. Dash to TJ's and put the kettle on!

- SCONES, TEA CAKES, AND OTHER SWEETS
- BRIOCHE BREAD LOAF (UNSLICED)

From the refrigerated section:

- WINE COUNTRY CHICKEN SALAD, ROSEMARY APRICOT CHICKEN SALAD, RANCHERO EGG WHITE SALAD, FOR SANDWICHES
- CREAM CHEESE AND PERSIAN CUCUMBERS, FOR CUCUMBER SANDWICHES

GRAB & GO
TJ's to a "Tea"

Well, the beverage here is obvious. There are three shelves of tea choices at my local Joe's. They include English or Irish Breakfast, Earl Grey, many non-caffeinated varieties, Jasmine Pearls, and several chais. If it's too hot for brewed tea, there are bottled brewed teas to serve iced, as well.

TJ'S THANKSGIVING

- ○ AUTUMN SALAD
- ○ CHERIE'S FAMILY EATS THIS DRESSING
- ○ SWEET POTATO PURÉE WITH CIDER REDUCTION
- ○ PECAN GREEN BEANS
- ○ CRANBERRY-GINGER PINOT NOIR SAUCE
- ○ TURKEY 411

Cooking the Thanksgiving feast generally requires lists of lists, a full day of prep, and setting the alarm for 0-dark:30 to start the bird. After years of teaching turkey classes and then celebrating with several family branches, the last thing I wanted to do was start the whole process once again. But my family loves to gather around the table with our own traditional favorites, so what was I to do? Go to TJ's, of course, and cook the whole meal from their ingredients. Ask your guests to bring dessert—you've done enough!

AUTUMN SALAD

The dressing in this beautiful, multi-hued salad gets its tang from the cranberry juice and vinegar, and its sweetness from the maple syrup, resulting in a forkful of flavor.

DRESSING:

2 tablespoons cranberry juice

2 tablespoons red wine vinegar

2 teaspoons maple syrup

1 teaspoon Dijon mustard

½ cup olive oil

salt and pepper

SALAD:

½ (7-ounce) bag arugula

½ (5-ounce) bag Trader Joe's Herb Salad Mix

1 pear or fuyu persimmon, sliced

2 ounces goat cheese

handful of dried cranberries

handful of pepitas

VEGETARIAN, GLUTEN-FREE

FOR DRESSING: Whisk together the cranberry juice, vinegar, maple syrup, and mustard. Stream in the olive oil, whisking constantly. Season to taste with salt and pepper.

FOR SALAD: Toss the arugula and herb salad with some of the dressing and arrange on plates or a platter. Arrange the pear or persimmon slices on top, and crumble the cheese over the salad. Scatter dried cranberries and pepitas (roasted pumpkin seeds) over the top, and drizzle with a little more dressing.

Prep Time: 10 minutes

GRAB & GO
No-Prep TJ's Thanksgiving

It's possible to grab the whole Thanksgiving feast from TJ's. Soup to turkey to nuts—the full meal is available to assemble and serve.

- MASHED POTATOES
- HARICOTS VERTS (FRENCH GREEN BEANS)
- CRANBERRY SAUCES
- DESSERTS

CHERIE'S FAMILY EATS this DRESSING

What's the difference between stuffing and dressing? My opinion is this: Stuffing is stuffed inside the bird, and dressing is cooked on the side. These days, I usually go the dressing route. The bird takes less time to cook when it's not stuffed, you don't have to worry about the internal temperature of the stuffing, and you can pop the casserole into the oven once the bird is out and resting.

6 cups cornbread
(day old is good)

½ pound Trader Joe's
Smoked Apple Chardonnay
Chicken Sausage (or any other
sausage you like)

4 ounces butter

1 large onion, chopped

3 ribs celery, chopped

½ cup dried apricots,
coarsely chopped

½ cup dried cherries

1 cup pecans, toasted
and coarsely chopped

½ cup chopped fresh herbs
(parsley, thyme, a little fresh
sage, a little fresh rosemary)

1 cup chicken or turkey broth

DO AHEAD

Preheat oven to 350°F. Crumble the cornbread into about 1½-inch cubes (this is a general size guideline—no rulers, please!). Scatter on a sheet pan and place in oven until bread has dried out slightly, 10 to 15 minutes, depending on how moist the bread is. The cubes should not be crispy, but just dry enough to be able to absorb the flavors of the other ingredients. Remove from oven and allow to cool to room temperature.

In a large sauté pan, crumble the sausage and cook until no longer pink. Remove sausage with a slotted spoon, reserving the drippings in the sauté pan. Add the sausage to the cornbread and set aside.

In the same sauté pan, melt the butter with the drippings (if the sausage was quite high in fat, you may want to reduce the amount of butter), and when it's sizzling, sauté the onion and celery until aromatic and slightly translucent. Add the chopped apricots, cherries, and pecans and cook until softened, about 3 minutes. Place this mixture in with the bread cubes, and allow to cool to room temperature. Toss the ingredients to mix them evenly, adding the herbs as you toss. Add as much chicken broth as you need to moisten the cornbread and season to taste with salt and freshly ground black pepper. (You may not need all the broth, depending on the amount of moisture in the bread and the amount of fat in the sausage.)

Place in an ovenproof casserole dish and bake, covered, until warmed through. Uncover, and bake about 15 minutes until top is crispy. (If you like it very crispy, don't cover the stuffing at all while it's in the oven.)

Prep Time: 20 minutes
Cooking Time: 45 minutes

If you decide to go the stuffing route, instead of cooking the dressing in a casserole, see my Turkey 411 tips (page 216) for a great way to line the cavity with cheesecloth, which allows you to pull the stuffing out easily and neatly.

SWEET POTATO PURÉE *with* CIDER REDUCTION

This recipe can go two ways—as a first-course soup or as a side dish. In a pinch, you can use canned sweet potato or butternut squash purée. A can and a half should do the trick.

2½ pounds sweet potatoes, peeled and cubed

2 cups Trader Joe's Spicy Cider

1 tablespoon minced fresh ginger

2 tablespoons butter

salt, pepper, and Trader Joe's Chili Pepper Hot Sauce or Jalapeño Pepper Hot Sauce

mascarpone and cubed pancetta, for garnish, optional

DO AHEAD
VEGETARIAN *(if made without pancetta garnish)*, **GLUTEN-FREE**

Place the sweet potatoes in a large saucepan, cover with water (or vegetable or chicken broth), and bring to a boil. Simmer until the potatoes are tender, 15 to 20 minutes. While the potatoes cook, simmer the cider in a medium sauté pan until syrupy and reduced to about ½ cup. When the potatoes are tender, drain them. Place the ginger, sweet potatoes, butter, and the cider syrup in a food processor and purée. Season to taste with salt, pepper, and hot sauce. Garnish with a small dollop of mascarpone and a little cubed pancetta, if desired.

Prep Time: 15 minutes
Cooking Time: 20 minutes

If making soup, reserve the cooking liquid from the sweet potatoes. Once the sweet potatoes are puréed, add the cooking liquid until the soup is of desired consistency.

PECAN GREEN BEANS

Simple and tasty—if you can't live without them, scatter Fried Onion Pieces over the top of the green beans for some crunchy, oniony goodness.

1 pound green (or green and yellow) beans, cooked crisp-tender

½ cup pecan halves

2 tablespoons red wine vinegar

½ cup olive (or canola) oil

salt and freshly ground black pepper

DO AHEAD *(pecan vinaigrette)*
VEGAN, GLUTEN-FREE

In a small sauté pan, toast the pecan halves (see Techniques section). Remove about 2 tablespoons and set aside. Place the rest of the pecans in a food processor or blender. Add the vinegar and blend. Add the oil in a steady stream while the motor is running. Toss the dressing with the beans and season to taste with salt and pepper. Garnish with reserved chopped pecans.

Prep Time: 5 minutes
Cooking Time: 10 minutes

CRANBERRY-GINGER PINOT NOIR SAUCE

I can't have too many cranberry sauce recipes, and this one is a keeper. The gingery notes really brighten up the flavor of the sauce. Hoard a few bags of cranberries during their short season—just toss the bags into the freezer, as is.

1 tablespoon butter

1 shallot, minced

2 cups cranberries

1 tablespoon fresh ginger, grated

2 cups Pinot Noir

1½ cups sugar

2 tablespoons candied ginger, chopped

salt and pepper

DO AHEAD
VEGETARIAN, GLUTEN-FREE

Melt butter in medium sauté pan. Sauté shallots until they soften, about 6 minutes. Add cranberries and grated ginger, and sauté until the berries have mostly popped, about 3 minutes. Add wine and sugar and bring to a boil. Boil until reduced by half, about 15 minutes. Remove from heat and add candied ginger. Season to taste with salt and pepper.

Prep Time: 5 minutes
Cooking Time: 20 minutes

TURKEY 411

TJ carries brined and unbrined fresh turkeys around the holidays. I'm a brined-turkey fan, and for many years, I brined my own. Not anymore—one TJ's-brined turkey was all it took to convert me. So easy and so delish! Here are my turkey tips for glorious, golden, roasted goodness.

APPROXIMATE ROASTING TIMES

12- to 16-pound unstuffed turkey at 350°F 2 to 2 ½ hours

16- to 20-pound unstuffed turkey at 350°F 3 to 3½ hours

12- to 16-pound stuffed turkey at 350°F 2½ to 3 hours

16- to 20-pound stuffed turkey at 350°F 3½ to 4 hours

Preheat the oven to 350°F. Remove the turkey from the refrigerator 30 to 60 before minutes cooking, so it can come (close to) room temperature. Rinse the turkey in cold water and remove the neck and giblets from the cavities. (Clean the sink well before and after you do this to avoid contamination from the raw poultry juices.) Pat dry. Season the bird as desired—don't salt a brined bird.

If you're stuffing the turkey, soak some cheesecloth in butter or chicken broth and line the cavity with this, then loosely fill it with room-temperature stuffing. (The cheesecloth will allow you to remove the stuffing neatly and easily.)

Place the turkey on a rack in a roasting pan. Pour about 1½ cups of water or chicken broth in the bottom of the pan and place the turkey in the oven. Roast at 350°F until the internal temperature reaches 140°F in the deepest part of the thigh, rotating the pan in the oven halfway through the total cooking time. (Be sure the meat thermometer is not touching bone, as that will throw off the reading.) Increase the oven temperature to 400°F in order to brown the skin. Roast until meat thermometer reads 155°F. (If you stuff the turkey, the stuffing should be 165°F in the center.) Cooking times will vary, depending upon how cold the turkey was when you began roasting. Remove the turkey from the oven, loosely cover with foil, and let rest at least 20 minutes before carving. The turkey's internal temperature will continue to rise, as the meat still cooks as it rests. The final temperature should be 165°F.

HOLIDAY PARTY

- ○ BRIE AND PEAR GALETTE
- ○ POTATO AND CHILE CRÈME SOUP
- ○ FETA-STUFFED MINI PEPPERS
- ○ CRANBERRY-PECAN TORTA
- ○ DATE KISSES

Once the jack-o'-lanterns shrivel, all we seem to schedule at my cooking school are appetizer classes. Everyone is looking for something to take to the holiday open houses, office parties, and get-togethers. Each of these recipes is easy to make and will be gobbled up fast. Better make a double batch! Of course, Trader Joe's stocks oodles of appetizers in the frozen section, especially at holiday time. So if time is short, make one or two of these and grab the rest from Joe's!

BRIE *and* PEAR GALETTE

This recipe from The I Love Trader Joe's Cookbook *has garnered the most raves from folks I've met. It's so delicious that people make it for parties all the time, and it's so easy that once you've made it once or twice, you won't need to pull out the recipe anymore. Switch it up with different cheese or with some minced rosemary. Make it your favorite, too!*

1 Trader Joe's Gourmet Pie Crust, thawed and rolled out to ¼-inch thickness (refreeze the remaining one for another use)

4 ounces Brie (rind removed), cubed

1 pear, thinly sliced

½ cup pecans, coarsely chopped

freshly ground black pepper

DO AHEAD
VEGETARIAN

Preheat oven to 375°F. Place the pie dough on a baking sheet and scatter half of the Brie over the center, leaving the edges clean. Arrange the sliced pears on top of the Brie. Scatter the pecans on top, and then add the remaining Brie. Fold the edges of the dough in to create a "picture frame" around the filling and bake 20 to 25 minutes, until crust is golden. Cut into wedges or squares to serve.

Prep Time: 10 minutes
Cooking Time: 25 minutes

POTATO AND CHILE CRÈME SOUP

Soup "shooters," served in espresso cups or shot glasses, became popular party fare a few years back. I'm a big fan of the trend. Especially for a winter soirée, a few sips of warm, comforting soup can really hit the spot. Crate and Barrel or Pier 1 usually carries inexpensive sets of the small glasses at holiday time.

1 tablespoon butter

1 tablespoon olive oil

1 cup chopped onion

2 cubes frozen garlic

2 (4-ounce) can Hatch Valley Diced Green Chiles

½ cup shredded carrot

4 cups vegetable broth

1 russet potato, peeled and cubed

½ cup crème fraîche

salt and pepper

Trader Joe's Spicy Shredded Cheese Blend, for garnish

DO AHEAD
VEGETARIAN

In a large saucepan, heat the butter and olive oil, and sauté the onion until it's fragrant and starts to soften, 3 to 4 minutes. Add the garlic and sauté 2 minutes until fragrant. Add the chopped chiles and carrot, and saute 3 to 4 minutes, until softened. Pour in the vegetable broth and bring to a boil. Add potato cubes and reduce heat to a simmer. Season lightly with salt and pepper. Simmer until potatoes are tender, about 20 minutes. Using an immersion blender or food processor, purée the soup. (If you use a food processor, strain the soup, reserving both the liquid and solids. Place the solids in the food processor, with just enough liquid to purée them. Return the solids to the pan, and add the remaining liquid.)

Add the crème fraîche and adjust seasoning to taste. Garnish with shredded cheese.

Prep Time: 15 minutes
Cooking Time: 30 minutes

The recipe makes enough for four regular (bowl-sized) servings, so depending on the size of your "shooters," you may have leftovers—not a bad thing!

FETA-STUFFED MINI PEPPERS

These are so pretty, and they taste even better than they look.

3 ounces feta cheese

2 ounces cream cheese

1 egg

1 teaspoon flour

2 tablespoons Trader Giotto's Genova Pesto (in the refrigerated section)

squeeze of fresh lemon juice

¼ cup crabmeat, optional

2 dozen Trader Joe's Minisweet Bell Peppers

fresh basil leaves, chiffonaded, for garnish (see Techniques)

DO AHEAD
(up to the point of baking)
VEGETARIAN *(if no crab used)*

Preheat oven to 400°F. In a food processor or the bowl of an electric mixer, combine the feta and cream cheese. Mix in the egg, flour, and pesto. Add a squeeze of lemon juice—about a teaspoon. Mix in the crab, if using. Lay a mini pepper on a cutting board, and cut a "flap" from the tip toward the stem. Transfer the feta mixture to a piping bag with a small, plain tip (or use a plastic bag), and pipe filling into each pepper. As you fill the peppers, place them on a parchment-lined baking sheet. When all the peppers are filled, bake for 20 to 25 minutes, until filling is set. Sprinkle with basil for garnish.

Prep Time: 10 minutes
Cooking Time: 30 minutes

CRANBERRY-PECAN TORTA

This is one of the most popular holiday appetizers from my cooking school. It looks gorgeous, holiday-ready, and like you've gone to more trouble than you actually have...who doesn't appreciate that in an appetizer?

1 pound cream cheese,
at room temperature

8 ounces mascarpone,
at room temperature

1 shallot, finely chopped

¼ cup chopped chives

salt and pepper

1 cup pecans,
toasted and chopped

1 cup cranberry sauce
(TJ's carries several each
holiday season,
both refrigerated and jarred)

DO AHEAD
VEGETARIAN, GLUTEN-FREE

Line a 4-cup bowl or mold with plastic wrap. Combine the cream cheese, mascarpone, chopped shallot, and chives, and season with salt and pepper. Place half the pecans in the bottom of the bowl and top with half the cream cheese mixture, spreading evenly. Place the cranberry sauce on top of the cream cheese, then add the remaining pecans. Top with remaining cream cheese mixture and cover with plastic wrap. Refrigerate at least 2 hours before unmolding.

Serve with crackers, sliced apples, pears, or fuyu persimmons.

Prep Time: 10 minutes
Chilling Time: 2 hours

DATE KISSES

Sweet, chewy fruit stuffed with salty cheese and crunchy almonds, wrapped in slightly crisped prosciutto...what's not to like?

8 Fancy Medjool Dates

1 ounce Manchego cheese

8 Marcona almonds or Trader
Joe's Spicy and Tangy Almonds

4 slices prosciutto,
cut in half lengthwise

Use a paring knife to remove the pits from the dates. Cut the cheese into small cubes, and fit one into the center of each date. Put an almond into the center of each date, and wrap each date in a half-strip of prosciutto. Heat a small sauté pan and brown the date kisses on all sides.

Prep Time: 5 minutes
Cooking Time: 5 minutes

You can pass on the pork to please vegetarian pals. In a pinch, you can skip the pan-searing. They'll still be tasty morsels of goodness.

⊙ APPENDIX

TECHNIQUES

Since you can't all come to Chez Cherie to learn all the secrets I pass along in my Trader Joe's classes, here's a short course on techniques mentioned in this book, from A to Z. Some of you may already be familiar with these techniques, but you never know, you might pick up some culinary-school lore to add a little pizzazz to your cooking!

AL DENTE—The key to perfect pasta, this term means "to the tooth," and describes that tiny bit of resistance that remains in the noodle after it's properly cooked. Because pasta continues to cook a little bit as you drain it and before it's sauced, when you bite into a piece to check doneness, there should be a tiny bit of tooth resistance. But no crunch! Practice makes perfect here, and pasta practice is never a bad thing!

BLIND BAKING—This method of preparing pie crust helps ensure a crisp bottom crust and is also done for pies with unbaked fillings, like a fruit tart filled with pastry cream. Here's how to do it: Preheat the oven to 375°F. Roll out the pie dough and fit it into an 8- or 9-inch pie pan or removable-bottom tart pan. Cover the pastry with a sheet of parchment that you've crumpled and then straightened out. (The wrinkles help the parchment form to the contours of the baking pan.) You can use aluminum foil instead of parchment, but don't use waxed paper. Cover the surface with pie weights, raw rice, or dried beans. (You'll need about 2 cups of raw dried beans or rice; you can reuse them a few times before they start to smell a bit baked.) Place the pan in the oven for 12 minutes. Carefully lift out the parchment, with the weights inside, and return the pan to the oven for 5 to 10 minutes, until the pastry is dry and golden. If you'll be adding a filling that goes back in the oven, underbake the pastry a bit; if the filling won't be baked, bake the pastry until it is completely done and beautifully browned.

CHIFFONADE—Just a chef-y word for thin ribbons, usually of herbs. To make them, stack up a few leaves (of basil, for example) and then roll them, as you would a stack of paper, into a scroll. Starting at one end of the roll, glide your knife through the rolled-up leaves, slicing them into thin ribbons. When you reach the end of the roll, fluff the pile of sliced leaves to separate them. Voila! Pretty and fragrant basil chiffonade, perfect for garnishing many dishes that would benefit from a scattering of tasty green ribbons.

DEGLAZE—This process incorporates all the lovely bits of food that have developed on the bottom of a sauté pan into the sauce. It's usually accomplished by adding a slightly acidic liquid (wine, anyone?) to the pan and stirring gently with a spatula until the bottom of the pan is clean and the flavorful stuff that was lurking there has been loosened. If you prefer to use broth for this rather than wine, a drop or two of lemon juice or vinegar will help the process along. You shouldn't need to scrape the pan with the spatula. Just stir gently after the liquid comes to a simmer and all should be well.

DEVEIN—If your shrimp don't already come deveined, it's a simple process. If the shrimp are already peeled, just stick the tip of a knife under the thin, dark line that extends down the back of the shrimp. Lift the membrane out and discard. If the shrimp have the shell intact, use a thin-bladed knife or kitchen shears to split the shell along the top edge (not where the little fringe-like "legs" are located). Peel the shell off, and then use the technique above to pull the vein out. That little black vein is harmless but it can contain sandy bits that won't complement your saffron crème sauce!

JULIENNE—This technique produces those thin strips or sticks you see in the restaurants without a lot of work. By cutting thick strips of vegetables or meat and then stacking a few of those strips and gliding your chef's knife through them again (the long way), you'll get thinner strips. Need even thinner ones? Just stack and glide again. (Kinda the "lather, rinse, repeat" of the kitchen!) Until your knife skills are rocking, don't make the stacks too high. Better to be safe than get stitches.

SAUTÉ—Technically, this means to make the food *jump* in the pan, with that impressive arc, like TV chefs do. In our Chez Cherie Basic Cooking series, we encourage students to practice this with a snack-size resealable plastic bag half-full of M&Ms. Once they've mastered the flip (in a room-temperature pan, of course—a hot pan would make this whole thing impossible!), they get to try it with loose candies. Muuuch harder, but I tell them they can eat the ones that jump out! If you want to skip this exercise, you can just use tongs or a spatula to get the food moving in the pan. The main idea is for the food to cook on all sides, so whether flipping, nudging, or turning it over with a spatula, the end result will be the same. I usually prefer a regular pan, not a non-stick pan, for sautéing because the untreated surface seems to heat faster and more evenly, allowing that lovely film of flavor to develop on the bottom of the pan (see *deglaze*).

SEGMENTING OR SUPRÉMING CITRUS—This is a fancier presentation for citrus than wedges, and requires a bit more time and practice, but it's a good skill to have in the kitchen arsenal. Start by cutting small slices off both ends of the citrus, and stand the fruit on a cutting board. Using a sharp paring knife, follow the curve of the fruit as you cut a swath of rind off, working from the top to the bottom. Continue around the fruit, trying to take all of the rind and as much of the pith as possible with each cut, but not too much of the flesh. Then turn the fruit over and make a second pass, removing any remaining spots of bitter pith. Now hold the fruit in your hand and take a look to determine where the lines of the membrane are. Cut just to one side of one segment, from the outside of the fruit in toward the center. Remove your knife, and do the same thing on the other side of that segment, completing a V-shaped cut. Lift the segment from the membrane. Keep working your way around the fruit, removing the segments one by one. Once you're done, give the membrane a good squeeze to get the last drops of juice. Use the juice in the recipe, if juice is called for, or drizzle it into your champagne!

TOASTING NUTS—While it's not absolutely essential, toasting nuts creates a wonderful depth of flavor that makes it worth doing. I *always* toast nuts in a sauté pan, *never* in the oven. Why? Because I like to stand at the stove with that sauté pan in one hand and practice my sautéing skills (see *sauté*) for the few moments it takes to make those nuts smell fragrant. That fragrance is the indication that the oil hiding in the nuts has been activated, and the nuts will taste *nuttier* for those few minutes in the pan. Why not the oven? Because then I'm no longer needed to stand and sauté, which means I invariably go off to do something else while the nuts toast away in the oven. By the time I smell the toasting nuts and remember that I stashed them in the oven, frequently they have, shall we say, "overtoasted"? Yeah, they've burned, and I need to start over.

ZESTING—The outer, colored part of citrus fruit is filled with fabulous flavor and citrus oil. It's rather inconveniently located on top of the bitter-tasting white pith. To remove just the colorful, tasty part—the zest—you'll need a kitchen tool. My very favorite tool for the job is a Microplane zester. These look kind of like a toothy metal ruler, and they remove the zest so efficiently that they would be worth the ten- to twenty-dollar investment even if that were their only use. But they also work wonderfully for grating chocolate, Parmesan cheese, nutmeg, and ginger. I think any well-equipped kitchen should contain one. If you're Microplane-less, a small bartender's tool called a zester will do the job, but you may need to chop the long strands that result. To use either, hold the fruit in your nondominant hand. (I'm a lefty, so the lemon goes in my right hand.) Then, wielding the grater or zester in your other (dominant) hand, run the teeth of the Microplane or the little holed edge of the zester over the surface of the citrus fruit, back and forth, until you have a gloriously fragrant pile of colorful fluff. That's the zest, and you'll be amazed at the flavor impact a pinch of that stuff will have on your food!

HOARDABLES AND PANTRY STAPLES

We all know that TJ's shelves are full of great stuff, but some items tend to disappear faster than a teenager when the dishwasher needs loading! This is a list of my current must-haves. Some items are seasonal, so I'll stockpile a year's worth of those when I can. (Organic canned pumpkin saved my reputation last year when I fielded a call from a frantic student whose family was counting on a big pot of pumpkin–black bean soup from *The I Love Trader Joe's Cookbook*. I met her at the cooking school with two cans in hand, saving her day and endearing myself to her forever!) Some items are perishable, so I just keep one container in the fridge, while others are shelf-stable, so I like to have four or five jars of those in my pantry at all times. You never know when the supply might be interrupted or a shortage might occur. There is a great sense of comfort to be derived from a well-stocked pantry and a full fridge, and you can create brilliant dishes on the fly if you have some of these hoardables on hand. Take a spin around your kitchen and see what you can come up with from the pantry and refrigerator shelves. Not only that, but if one of your favorite things disappears from the TJ's shelf completely, at least you'll have some of it in reserve so you can wean yourself off it slowly. (I still have one jar of my beloved vanilla paste in my cupboard, but I'm reluctant to use it all up!) You've probably got a hoardables list of your own, but if not, here's mine to get you started.

ACE'S PEAR CIDER

AIOLI GARLIC MUSTARD SAUCE

BALSAMIC VINEGAR

BLACK BELUGA LENTILS *(vacuum packaged)*

BLACK EYED PEAS *(refrigerated)*

BLACK PEPPER SAUCE

BLACKTHORN FERMENTED CIDER

BROWNIE TRUFFLE BAKING MIX

BUTTERMILK BISCUITS *(refrigerated)*

CALIFORNIA ESTATE OLIVE OIL

CANDIED GINGER

CAPERS IN VINEGAR *(in a jar)*

CARNITAS *(refrigerated)*

CHERRIES, DRIED

CHERRY PRESERVES

CHICKEN SAVORY BROTH CONCENTRATE

CILANTRO ROASTED PECAN DIP *(refrigerated)*

COCONUT MILK *(canned)*

CORN AND CHILE TOMATO-LESS SALSA

CORNICHONS

CRABMEAT *(canned, refrigerated)*

CRANBERRIES, FRESH *(seasonal, in produce aisle—freeze in the bag for use all year)*

CRÈME FRAÎCHE

CROISSANTS *(frozen)*

DIJON MUSTARD

EDAMAME, SHELLED *(refrigerated)*

EGGPLANT CAPONATA *(in a jar)*

FARFALLE PASTA

FROZEN GARLIC CUBES

GENERAL TSAO STIR-FRY SAUCE

GOAT CHEESE *(Trader Joe's Chèvre, Madame Chèvre, or Silver Goat Chèvre)*

GOURMET CHICKEN MEATBALLS WITH SUN-DRIED TOMOATOES, BASIL, AND PROVELONE

GOURMET FRIED ONION PIECES

GRAPESEED OIL

GREEK-STYLE FAGE TOTAL YOGURT

GREEN OLIVE TAPENADE

HARVEST GRAINS BLEND

HATCH VALLEY FIRE-ROASTED DICED GREEN CHILES

HEAVY CREAM

INDIAN FARE DAL MAKHANI

ISRAELI COUSCOUS

JUST ALMOND MEAL

LEMON CURD *(in a jar)*

LEMON PEPPER PAPPARADELLE PASTA

LIMONCELLO

MÂCHE LETTUCE

MANGO-GINGER CHUTNEY

MAPLE SYRUP *(Grade B)*

MARCONA ALMONDS

MASCARPONE

MEDJOOL DATES

MINI BURGER BUNS

MINI MILK CHOCOLATE PEANUT BUTTER CUPS

MIXED WILD MUSHROOM MEDLEY *(dried)*

MULTIGRAIN BAKING AND PANCAKE MIX

NIMAN RANCH APPLEWOOD SMOKED DRY-CURED BACON

ORANGE MUSCAT CHAMPAGNE VINEGAR

ORGANIC POLENTA

ORGANIC PUMPKIN PURÉE *(canned, seasonal—holiday)*

ORGANIC QUINOA

PANCETTA, CUBED

PANKO BREAD CRUMBS

PEPITAS *(roasted pumpkin seeds)*

PIQUILLO PEPPERS *(roasted, in a jar)*

PIZZA DOUGH *(refrigerated)*

POMEGRANATE ARILS *(seasonal)*

POUND PLUS CHOCOLATE BARS

PROSCIUTTO

PULLED PORK IN SMOKY BBQ SAUCE

PUMPKIN BREAD AND MUFFIN MIX *(seasonal—holiday)*

PUMPKIN BUTTER *(seasonal—holiday)*

RATATOUILLE *(in a jar)*

RED CHILE PEPPER FLAKES

RED WINE VINEGAR

RICE VINEGAR

RICES: BASMATI, JASMINE, ARBORIO, WILD

ROASTED CORN *(frozen)*

ROSEMARY PECANS AND CRANBERRIES

SATAY PEANUT SAUCE

SEAFOOD SAUSAGES *(frozen)*

SHALLOTS

SMOKED TROUT IN OLIVE OIL *(canned)*

SOFT LADY FINGERS *(seasonal—holiday)*

SPANISH SAFFRON

SPARKLING LEMONADE

SPICY BROWN MUSTARD

SPICY CHAI LATTE MIX

SPICY, SMOKY PEACH SALSA *(in a jar)*

SWEET CHILI SAUCE

SWEETENED CONDENSED MILK

TACO SEASONING MIX

TEENY TINY POTATOES

THAI-STYLE RICE STICKS

TRADER GIOTTO'S GENOVA PESTO *(refrigerated)*

TRADER GIOTTO'S ORGANIC VODKA PASTA SAUCE

TRADER JOE'S GOURMET PIE CRUST *(frozen, seasonal—holiday)*

TRIPLE GINGER SNAPS

TURBINADO SUGAR

VANILLA CAKE AND BAKING MIX

VERMOUTH, DRY

WASABI MAYONNAISE

WHOLE WHEAT COUSCOUS

CONVERSIONS

MEASURE	EQUIVALENT	METRIC
1 teaspoon		5.0 milliliters
1 tablespoon	3 teaspoons	14.8 milliliters
1 cup	16 tablespoons	236.8 milliliters
1 pint	2 cups	473.6 milliliters
1 quart	4 cups	947.2 milliliters
1 liter	4 cups + 3½ tablespoons	1000 milliliters
1 ounce (dry)	2 tablespoons	28.35 grams
1 pound	16 ounces	453.49 grams
2.21 pounds	35.3 ounces	1 kilogram

PHOTO CREDITS

Photos on pages 15, 18, 25, 26, 31, 32, 37, 39, 46, 49, 53, 55, 58, 62, 67, 69, 72, 77, 78, 84, 87, 91, 95, 99, 103, 107, 109, 115, 119, 123, 126, 131, 134, 139, 143, 145 (shortcake), 146, 149, 153, 155, 157, 163, 165, 168, 170, 176, 179, 181, 186, 189, 193, 198, 201, 202, 204, 209, 213, 217, 222, 224 © Kevin Twohy. All other photos are from shutterstock.com:

p. 12: cabbage © dimon75; champagne © haveseen; pear © Doris Rich; tangerine © mimo

p. 20: © nicobatista

p. 21: baguette © grintan; eggplant © Yaroslava; pasta © pinkkoala; strainer © dimon75

p. 28: grintan

p. 29: beer © Doris Rich; cheese and onions © Kevin Twohy; chips © Picsfive

p. 35: bamboo © olives; lilypad © Roberto castillo; rice © Roxana Bashyrova; wasabi © Alexander Ilin

p. 42: © Gordan Gledec

p. 43: cherries 0legik; pistachios © geniuscook_com

p. 44: © Barbara Delgado

p. 50: © Vasil Vasilev

p. 51: bananas © Kletr; shrimp © svariophoto

p. 57: film © Dolly; ice cream M. Unal Ozmen; pasta © Beat Bieler

p. 61: © Laura Gangi Pond

p. 65: chile © cameilia; corn © testing; sandwich © Vinata

p. 73: cabbage © marylooo; clover © Roberto castillo; crab © Graphic design; horseshoe © caramelina; shamrock © caramelina; snake © ananas

p. 74: Elena Elisseeva

p. 80: Sergey Peterman

p. 81: cheese © Brian Weed; grapes © marinamik; mushrooms © Goran Kuzmanovski; wine © Marijus Auruskevicius

p. 82: © Kenishirotie

p. 89: asparagus © camellia; berries © Pinkcandy; fish © AKaiser; fruit bowl © Doris Rich

p. 93: © Alex Staroseltsev

p. 96: © GrigoryL

p. 97: avocado © Doris Rich; cactus © vdLee; cilantro © Simone Voigt; leaf © sergwsq; Mayan calendar Lukiyanova Natalia / frental; salsa © Greenfire

p. 105: almonds © marco mayer; boots © Mikateke; cucumber © L_amica; onion © Tatik22; picnic basket © Dolly

p. 111: © bonchan

p. 112: Valentyn Volkov

p. 113: glasses © dimon75; lemon © S1001; martini © gresei; olives © Barbro Bergfeldt

p. 117: © DFabri

p. 120: ampFotoStudio

p. 121: bowl and whisk © Roberto castillo; bacon © ElliotKo; grapefruit © grocap; leaves © sergwsq

p. 129: artichoke © Sally Scott; bullfighter © Alvaro Cabrera Jimenez; horse © Alvaro Cabrera Jimenez; orange © Doris Rich

p. 137: coffee beans © Scorpp; grill © John T Takai; man © Doris Rich; tomatoes © silver-john

p. 144: David P. Smith

p. 145: basket © Brooke Fuller; crab © Pika

p. 151: corn © Kitch Bain; drum © Olga Rutko; flag © Vlue; peaches © Dino O

p. 158: © Evgeniya Uvarova

p. 159: cheese © Gregory Gerber; Eiffel tower © Jiri Vaclavek; lettuce © Ivonne Wierink; mushrooms © -V-; pitcher © marinamik

p. 161: © Nattika

p. 167: ball, chair, and sunglasses © Canicula; mint © Subbotina Anna; watermelon © Anna Sedneva

p. 173: alejandro dans neergaard

p. 175: edamame © rodho; hair accoutrements © demon 75; strawberries © grublee

p. 182: © oksix

p. 183: butternut squash © Peter zijlstra; coconut © Pakimon; elephant © Elfwilde; flourish © sergwsq; Taj Mahal © RLN

p. 190: © DUSAN ZIDAR

p. 191: jack-o-lantern © Athos Boncompagni Illustratore; flower © Denis Barbulat; pumpkin © deniss09; skull © jumpingsack; witch hat © RamonaS

p. 196: © PeppPic

p. 197: eggs © gjfoto; number 1 © doodle; pennant © Pause; pig © Mila Petkova; rolls © robootb

p. 203: bouquet © Andre Blais; tea cup © marinamik; tea set © Leonid Yakutin

p. 206: © Olga Popova

p. 211: cornucopia © vectorkat; cranberries © mikie11; green beans © Tamara Kulikova; turkey © Mila Petkova

p. 219: brie © Richard Griffin; pears © Aleksandr Bryliaev

p. 220: © Peter zijlstra

RECIPE INDEX

INDEX

Major ingredients are indexed below.

ABOUT THE AUTHOR

© Yvette Sharis

Cherie Mercer Twohy is author of *The I Love Trader Joe's Cookbook*. Family and food are the touchstones in her life. After attending culinary school late in life, she found her bliss teaching cooking. Her cooking school, Chez Cherie, in La Canada, California (www.chezcherie.com), has hosted thousands of students since opening in 2000. Her husband and three children have served as (mostly) enthusiastic recipe-testers, for which they have her eternal gratitude. Twohy holds a Certified Culinary Professional (CCP) designation from the International Association of Culinary Professionals. Among her most prized possessions is an authentic Trader Joe's shirt, awarded to her by a Captain at one of her local Joe's. Cherie can be reached at cherie@ilovetraderjoes.com.